KING'S CROSS

ALSO BY TIMOTHY KELLER

The Reason for God: Belief in an Age of Skepticism

The Prodigal God: Recovering the Heart of the Christian Faith

Counterfeit Gods: The Empty Promises of Money, Sex, and Power, and the Only Hope That Matters

Generous Justice: How God's Grace Makes Us Just

KING'S CROSS

THE STORY OF THE WORLD IN
THE LIFE OF JESUS

TIMOTHY KELLER

DUTTON   REDEEMER

DUTTON
Published by Penguin Group (USA) Inc.
375 Hudson Street, New York, New York 10014, U.S.A.
Penguin Group (Canada), 90 Eglinton Avenue East, Suite 700, Toronto, Ontario M4P 2Y3,
Canada (a division of Pearson Penguin Canada Inc.); Penguin Books Ltd, 80 Strand, London
WC2R 0RL, England; Penguin Ireland, 25 St Stephen's Green, Dublin 2, Ireland (a division of
Penguin Books Ltd); Penguin Group (Australia), 250 Camberwell Road, Camberwell, Victoria
3124, Australia (a division of Pearson Australia Group Pty Ltd); Penguin Books India Pvt Ltd,
11 Community Centre, Panchsheel Park, New Delhi—110 017, India; Penguin Group (NZ),
67 Apollo Drive, Rosedale, North Shore 0632, New Zealand (a division of Pearson
New Zealand Ltd); Penguin Books (South Africa) (Pty) Ltd, 24 Sturdee Avenue,
Rosebank, Johannesburg 2196, South Africa

Penguin Books Ltd, Registered Offices: 80 Strand, London WC2R 0RL, England

Published by Dutton, a member of Penguin Group (USA) Inc.

First printing, February 2011
1   3   5   7   9   10   8   6   4   2

Copyright © 2011 by Redeemer CityNet and Timothy Keller
All rights reserved

Scriptures taken from the Holy Bible, *New International Version*®, NIV®. Copyright © 1973,
1978, 1984 by Biblica, Inc.™ Used by permission of Zondervan. All rights reserved worldwide.
The "NIV" and "New International Version" are trademarks registered in the
United States Patent and Trademark Office by Biblica, Inc.™

 REGISTERED TRADEMARK—MARCA REGISTRADA

LIBRARY OF CONGRESS CATALOGING-IN-PUBLICATION DATA

Keller, Timothy J., 1950–
King's cross : the story of the world in the life of Jesus / Timothy Keller.
p. cm.
ISBN 978-0-525-95210-7 (hardcover)
1. Jesus Christ—Person and offices—Biblical teaching.   2. Bible.
N.T. Mark—Criticism, interpretation, etc.   I. Title.
BT203.K444 2011
232'8—dc22
2010047356

Printed in the United States of America
Set in ITC Galliard
Designed by Leonard Telesca

To Scott Kauffmann and Sam Shammas, without whom this book would not exist

And also to the rest of the staff of Redeemer Presbyterian Church and Redeemer City to City—the Dream Team!—without whom not much else of our current ministry would exist

Thanks, all.

CONTENTS

Contents

PART TWO: THE CROSS

BEFORE

To my surprise, in recent decades the amount of attention the general culture gives to the historical Jesus has been increasing. Every year as Easter approaches, there are numerous media features about Jesus. This past Easter, *Newsweek* religion editor Lisa Miller explained that "Easter is . . . a celebration of the final act of the Passion, in which Jesus rose from his tomb in his body three days after his execution. . . . The Gospels insist on the veracity of this supernatural event. . . . Jesus died and rose again so that all his followers could, eventually, do the same. This story has strained the credulity of even the most devoted believer. For, truly, it's unbelievable."[1]

In his article "Myth or History: The Hard Facts of the Resurrection" for *The Times* (UK), Geza Vermes poses this question: "At the heart of the message of Christianity lies the resurrection of Jesus. The chief herald of this message, St. Paul, bluntly proclaims: 'If Christ has not been raised, your faith is futile.' How does his statement, reinforced by two millennia of theological

[*ix*]

cogitation, compare with what the Gospels tell us about the first Easter? Is it myth or does it contain a grain of history?"[2]

Nanci Hellmich reported in *USA Today* that "Two researchers analyzed the food and plate sizes in 52 of the most famous paintings of *The Last Supper* and found that the portion sizes in the paintings have increased dramatically over the past millennium."[3] The popular press has a lot to say about Jesus.

And of course, they aren't the only ones. It wouldn't be an exaggeration to say that the subject of Jesus is its own genre, featuring carefully researched biographies, scholarly textual commentaries, historical criticism, speculative fiction, antimythologies, and everything in between.

Into this seemingly inexhaustible current of words and thought about Jesus, I gingerly lay this volume. It is an extended meditation on the historical Christian premise that Jesus's life, death, and resurrection form the central event of cosmic and human history as well as the central organizing principle of our own lives. Said another way, the whole story of the world—and of how we fit into it—is most clearly understood through a careful, direct look at the story of Jesus. My purpose here is to try to show, through his words and actions, how beautifully his life makes sense of ours.

A True Life Story

If we want to investigate that life, to discern whether Jesus really did live and die and rise again, to know if the Easter story contains even "a grain of history" or perhaps even the key to history, we need to go to the Gospels, the historical documents that tell Jesus's story. These Gospels are named after their authors: Matthew, Mark, Luke, and John.

Much of the recent "Jesus genre" consists of argument over whether the Gospels are reliable records of Jesus's life. Two hundred years ago, some scholars began to propose that the Gospels were oral traditions embellished with many legendary elements over the generations, and were not written down until more than one hundred years after the events of Jesus's life.[4] These claims have convinced many people over the years that we cannot know who Jesus really was. German philosopher Friedrich Nietzsche and English author George Eliot lost hold of their Christian faith largely from reading the skeptical *Life of Jesus Critically Examined* by David Strauss, and each year thousands of students find their beliefs shaken in the same way by the typical undergraduate course in "the Bible as literature."

There is a countermovement going on, however. One hundred fifty years ago it was confidently asserted that no Gospel existed before the third decade of the second century A.D. But over the past century the evidence has become overwhelming that the Gospels were written down much earlier, within the lifetime of many of the eyewitnesses to Jesus's life and death.[5] This has led to "faith reversals," as in the well-publicized cases of Anne Rice and A. N. Wilson. The biographer Wilson wrote *Jesus: A Life* in 1992, which presupposed the thesis that the Gospels are nearly entirely legendary. Yet in 2009 he revealed how he had returned to Christian faith after years of atheism and of writing books assaulting Christianity.[6] Novelist Rice had lost her faith in college, but when she began to read the work of prominent Bible scholars, she discovered that:

> The whole case for the nondivine Jesus who stumbled into Jerusalem and somehow got crucified by nobody and had nothing to do with the founding of Christianity and would be horrified by it if he knew about

it—that whole picture which had floated in the liberal circles I frequented as an atheist for thirty years—that case was not made.[7]

Richard Bauckham's *Jesus and the Eyewitnesses* makes, I think, the most conclusive argument that the Gospels are not long-evolving oral traditions but rather oral *histories*, written down from the accounts of the eyewitnesses themselves who were still alive and active in the community.

Bauckham cites extensive evidence that for decades after Jesus's death and resurrection the people who were healed by Jesus, like the paralytic who was lowered through the roof; the person who carried the cross for Jesus, Simon of Cyrene; the women who watched Jesus being placed in the tomb, like Mary Magdalene; and the disciples who had followed Jesus for three years, like Peter and John—all of these participants in the life of Jesus continually and publicly repeated these incidents in great detail. For decades these eyewitnesses told the stories of what happened to them. Matthew, Mark, Luke, and John wrote down these accounts and so we have the Gospels.

Bauckham also observes that the Gospels are too counterproductive in their content to be legends. For example, it is astonishing that in the very foundational documents of the Christian church we would have a record that one of the greatest leaders of the church, Peter, was an enormous failure who even cursed Jesus in public. The only credible source for the account of Peter's denial and betrayal of Jesus would be Peter himself: No one else could have known the details we are given. And no one in the early church would have dared to highlight the weakness of its most revered and significant leader with such candor—unless that very weakness was an important part of the story. And unless, of course, the accounts were true.

The Gospel of Mark

For the purposes of this book, I sensed that the best way to explore the life of Jesus was not to make a survey of all the Gospels, but to examine a single, coherent narrative: one that focused intently on the actual words and actions (especially the actions) of Jesus. This led me to the Gospel of Mark.

Who was Mark? The earliest and most important source of an answer comes from Papias, bishop of Hierapolis until 130 A.D., who said that Mark had been a secretary and translator for Peter, one of the first twelve of Jesus's disciples or followers, and "wrote accurately all that [Peter] remembered." This testimony is of particular significance, since there is evidence that Papias (who lived from 60–135 A.D.) knew John, another of Jesus's first and closest disciples, personally.[8] Bauckham's volume demonstrates that, indeed, Mark mentions Peter proportionately more than any of the other Gospels. If you go through the book of Mark, you'll see that nothing happens in which Peter is not present. The entire Gospel of Mark, then, is almost certainly the eyewitness testimony of Peter.

There is another reason to base our life of Jesus on the Gospel of Mark. Mark does not read like a dry history. It is written in the present tense, often using words like "immediately" to pack the account full of action. You can't help but notice the abruptness and breathless speed of the narrative. This Gospel conveys, then, something important about Jesus. He is not merely a historical figure, but a living reality, a person who addresses us *today*. In his very first sentence Mark tells us that God has broken into history. His style communicates a sense of crisis, that the status quo has been ruptured. We can't think of history as a closed system of natural causes anymore. We can't think of any human system or tradition or authority as inevitable or absolute anymore.

Jesus has come; anything can happen now. Mark wants us to see that the coming of Jesus calls for decisive action. Jesus is seen as a man of action, moving quickly and decisively from event to event. There is relatively little of Jesus's *teaching* in the Gospel of Mark—mainly, we see Jesus *doing*. Therefore we can't remain neutral; we need to respond actively.

The King and the Cross

You may know King's Cross as a railway station in London, England, one that has been immortalized in the Harry Potter books. But it's such a perfect encapsulation of the meaning of Jesus's life that I couldn't resist borrowing it for the title of this book.

You see, the Gospel of Mark has one more feature that makes it ideal for our purposes here. Mark's account of Jesus's life is presented to us in two symmetrical acts: his *identity* as King over all things (in Mark chapters 1–8), and his *purpose* in dying on the cross (in Mark chapters 9–16).

This book's structure follows its title: two parts ("The King" and "The Cross"), each consisting of several chapters, with each chapter exploring a key part of this story told in Mark's Gospel.

All books are selective in what they include, including the Gospels themselves; John concludes his own Gospel with the words "Jesus did many other things as well. If every one of them were written down, I suppose that even the whole world would not have room for the books that would be written" (John 21:25). I have chosen to focus on a number of specific texts in Mark that I believe best trace the narrative of Jesus's life, or expand on the themes of his identity or purpose. This means a handful of well-known passages aren't addressed in detail in this book.

I trust that you will find the figure of Jesus worthy of your attention: unpredictable yet reliable, gentle yet powerful, authoritative yet humble, human yet divine. I urge you to seriously consider the significance of his life in your own.

Our True Life Story

Although I was raised in a Christian church, it was only in college that I found vital, life-changing faith in Jesus. One of the vehicles of that spiritual awakening was the Bible, especially the Gospel accounts in the New Testament. I had studied the Bible before. When I went through confirmation classes in my church, I had to memorize Scripture. But during college the Bible came alive in a way that was hard to describe. The best way I can put it is that, before the change, I pored over the Bible, questioning and analyzing it. But after the change it was as if the Bible, or maybe Someone through the Bible, began poring over me, questioning and analyzing me.

Not long after this happened to me, I came across an article in a magazine entitled "The Book That Understands Me," by Emile Cailliet, professor of philosophy at Princeton Theological Seminary.[9] In his college days in France, Cailliet had been an agnostic. He graduated from university without having ever actually seen a Bible. Then he served in the army during World War I. "The inadequacy of my views on the human situation overwhelmed me," he wrote. "What use . . . the philosophic banter of the seminar, when your own buddy—at the time speaking to you of his mother—dies standing in front of you, a bullet in his chest?"

Then a bullet got him as well, and he began recuperating during a long stay in a hospital. Reading literature and philosophy, he began strangely longing—"I must say it, however queer it may sound—for a book that would understand me." Since he knew of no such book, he decided to prepare one for himself. He read widely, and whenever he found a brief passage that particularly struck him and "spoke to my condition," he would carefully copy it down in a leather-bound pocket-size volume. As time went on and the number of quotations grew, he eagerly anticipated sitting down and reading it from cover to cover. He expected that "it would lead me as it were from fear and anguish, through a variety of intervening stages, to supreme utterances of release and jubilation."

One day he went out to sit under a tree in his garden to read his precious anthology. As he did so, a growing disappointment came over him. Each quote reminded him of the circumstances in which he had chosen it, but things had changed. "Then I knew that the whole undertaking would not work, simply because it was of my own making."

Almost at that very moment, his wife appeared after a walk with their child in a baby carriage. She had with her a Bible in French that she had received from a minister she had met on her walk. Cailliet took it and opened it to the Gospels. He continued to read deep into the night. The realization dawned on him: "Lo and behold, as I looked through them [the Gospels] the One who spoke and acted in them became alive to me. . . . This is the book that would understand me."[10]

Reading that article, I realized that the same thing had happened to me. Though as a youth I had believed that the Bible was the Word of the Lord, I had not personally met the Lord of the Word. As I read the Gospels, he became real to me. Thirty years later I preached through the book of Mark at my church in New York City, in the hope that many others would likewise find Jesus in the accounts of the Gospels.

This book is inspired by those sermons, and it is offered with the same aspiration for the readers.

PART ONE

THE KING
The Identity of Jesus

ONE

✦✦✦✦

THE DANCE

The beginning of the gospel about Jesus Christ, the Son of God.
It is written in Isaiah the prophet:
"I will send my messenger ahead of you, who will prepare your way"—"a voice of one calling in the desert,
'Prepare the way for the Lord, make straight paths for him.'"
And so John came, baptizing in the desert region and preaching.

(Mark 1:1–4)

Mark wastes no time in establishing the identity of his subject. He abruptly and bluntly asserts that Jesus is the "Christ" and the "Son of God." *Christos* was a Greek word meaning "an anointed royal figure." It was another way of referring to the "Messiah," the one who would come and administer

God's rule on earth, and rescue Israel from all its oppressors and troubles. Not just *a* king, but The King.

But Mark does not just call Jesus the "Christ"; he goes further. "Son of God" is an astonishingly bold term that goes beyond the popular understanding of the Messiah at the time. It is a claim of outright divinity. Mark then raises the stakes all the way and makes the ultimate claim. By quoting Isaiah's prophetic passage, Mark asserts that John the Baptist is the fulfillment of the "voice" calling out in the desert. Since Mark equates John with the one who would "prepare the way for the Lord," by clear inference it means he is equating Jesus with the Lord himself, with God Almighty. The Lord God; the long-awaited divine King who would rescue his people; and Jesus—they are somehow one and the same person.

In making this audacious claim, Mark roots Jesus as deeply as possible in the historic, ancient religion of Israel. Christianity, he implies, is not a completely new thing. Jesus is the fulfillment of all the biblical prophets' longings and visions, and he is the one who will come to rule and renew the entire universe.

The Dance of Reality

Having announced him in this way, Mark introduces Jesus in a striking scene that tells us more about his identity:

> *Jesus came from Nazareth in Galilee and was baptized by John in the Jordan. As Jesus was coming up out of the water, he saw heaven being torn open and the Spirit descending on him like a dove. And a voice came from heaven: "You are my Son, whom I love; with you I am well pleased."*

> (Mark 1:9–11)

For the Spirit of God to be pictured as a dove is not particularly striking to us, but when Mark was writing, it was very rare. In the sacred writings of Judaism there is only one place where the Spirit of God is likened to a dove, and that is in the Targums, the Aramaic translation of the Hebrew Scriptures that the Jews of Mark's time read. In the creation account, the book of Genesis 1:2 says that the Spirit *hovered* over the face of the waters. The Hebrew verb here means "flutter": the Spirit fluttered over the face of the waters. To capture this vivid image, the rabbis translated the passage for the Targums like this: "And the earth was without form and empty, and darkness was on the face of the deep, and the Spirit of God fluttered above the face of the waters *like a dove*, and God spoke: 'Let there be light.'" There are three parties active in the creation of the world: God, God's Spirit, and God's Word, through which he creates. The same three parties are present at Jesus's baptism: the Father, who is the voice; the Son, who is the Word; and the Spirit fluttering like a dove. Mark is deliberately pointing us back to the creation, to the very beginning of history. Just as the original creation of the world was a project of the triune God, Mark says, so the redemption of the world, the rescue and renewal of all things that is beginning now with the arrival of the King, is also a project of the triune God.

That's what Mark is doing with his picture of Jesus's baptism. But why is it important that creation and redemption are both products of a Trinity, one God in three persons?

The Christian teaching of the Trinity is mysterious and cognitively challenging. The doctrine of the Trinity is that God is one God, eternally existent in three persons. That's not tritheism, with three gods who work in harmony; neither is it unipersonalism, the notion that sometimes God takes one form and sometimes he takes another, but that these are simply different manifestations of one God. Instead, trinitarianism holds that there is one God in three persons who know and love one another. God is not more fundamentally one than he is three, and he is not more fundamentally three than he is one.

When Jesus comes out of the water, the Father envelops him and covers him with words of love: "You are my Son, whom I love; with you I am well pleased." Meanwhile the Spirit covers him with power. This is what has been happening in the interior life of the Trinity from all eternity. Mark is giving us a glimpse into the very heart of reality, the meaning of life, the essence of the universe. According to the Bible, the Father, the Son, and the Spirit glorify one another. Jesus says in his prayer recorded in John's Gospel: "I have brought you glory on earth by completing the work you gave me to do. And now, Father, glorify me in your presence with the glory that I had with you before the world began" (John 17:4–5). Each person of the Trinity glorifies the other.

In the words of my favorite author, C. S. Lewis, "In Christianity God is not a static thing . . . but a dynamic, pulsating activity, a life, almost a kind of drama. Almost, if you will not think me irreverent, a kind of dance."[11] Theologian Cornelius Plantinga develops this further, noting that the Bible says the Father, the Son, and the Spirit glorify one another: "The persons within God exalt each other, commune with each other, and defer to one another. . . . Each divine person harbors the others at the center of his being. In constant movement of overture and acceptance, each person envelops and encircles the others. . . . God's interior life [therefore] overflows with regard for others."[12]

You're glorifying something when you find it beautiful for what it is in itself. Its beauty compels you to adore it, to have your imagination captured by it. This happened to me with Mozart. I listened to Mozart to get an A in music appreciation in college.

I had to get good grades to get a good job, so in other words, I listened to Mozart to make money. But today I am quite willing to spend money just to listen to Mozart, not because it's useful to me anymore but because it's beautiful in itself. It's no longer a means to an end.

And when it's a person you find beautiful in that way, you want to serve them unconditionally. When you say, "I'll serve, as long as I'm getting benefits from it," that's not actually serving people; it's serving yourself through them. That's not circling them, orbiting around them; it's using them, getting them to orbit around you.

Of course there are many of us who *look* unselfish and dutiful, simply because we can't say no: We say yes to everything, and people are always using us. Everybody says, "Oh, you're so self-less, so giving of yourself; you need to think more about taking care of yourself." But think about those of us who don't have boundaries and who let people walk all over us and use us and can't say no—do you think we're doing that out of love for other people? Of course not, we're doing it out of *need*—we say yes to everything out of fear and cowardice. That's far from glorifying others. To glorify others means to unconditionally serve them, not because we're getting anything out of it, just because of our love and appreciation for who they truly are.

The Father, the Son, and the Spirit are each centering on the others, adoring and serving them. And because the Father, Son, and Spirit are giving glorifying love to one another, God is infinitely, profoundly happy. Think about this: If you find some-body you adore, someone for whom you would do anything, and you discover that this person feels the same way about you, does that feel good? It's sublime! That's what God has been enjoying for all eternity. The Father, the Son, and the Spirit are pour-ing love and joy and adoration into the other, each one serving the other. They are infinitely seeking one another's glory, and so God is infinitely happy. And if it's true that this world has been created by this triune God, then ultimate reality is a dance.

"What does it all matter?" Lewis writes. "It matters more than anything else in the world. The whole dance, or drama, or pattern of this three-Personal life is to be played out in each one of us. . . . [Joy, power, peace, eternal life] are a great fountain of energy and beauty spurting up at the very centre of reality."[13] Why does Lewis choose to dwell on the image of the dance? A self-centered life is a stationary life; it's static, not dynamic. A self-centered person wants to be the center around which everything else orbits. I might help people; I might have friends; I might fall in love as long as there's no compromise of my individual interests or whatever meets my needs. I might even give to the poor—as long as it makes me feel good about myself and doesn't hinder my lifestyle too much. Self-centeredness makes everything else a means to an end. And that end, that nonnegotiable, is whatever I want and whatever I like, my interests over theirs. I'll have fun with people, I'll talk with people, but in the end everything orbits around me.

If everyone is saying, "No, you orbit around *me*!" what happens? Picture five people, ten people, a hundred people on a stage together, and every one of them wants to be the center. They all just stand there and say to the others, "You move around me." And nobody gets anywhere; the dance becomes hazardous, if not impossible.

The Trinity is utterly different. Instead of self-centeredness, the Father, the Son, and the Spirit are characterized in their very essence by *mutually self-giving love.* No person in the Trinity insists that the others revolve around him; rather each of them voluntarily circles and orbits around the others.

Entering the Dance

If this is ultimate reality, if this is what the God who made the universe is like, then this truth bristles and explodes with life-shaping, glorious implications for us. *If this world was made by a triune God, relationships of love are what life is really all about.*

You see, different views of God have different implications. If there's no God—if we are here by blind chance, strictly as a result of natural selection—then what you and I call love is just a chemical condition of the brain. Evolutionary biologists say there's nothing in us that isn't there because it helped our ancestors pass on the genetic code more successfully. If you feel love, it's only because that combination of chemicals enables you to survive and gets your body parts in the places they need to be in order to pass on the genetic code. That's all love is—chemistry. On the other hand, if God exists but is unipersonal, there was a time when God was not love. Before God created the world, when there was only one divine person, there was no lover, because love can exist only in a relationship. If a unipersonal God had created the world and its inhabitants, such a God would not in his essence be love. Power and greatness possibly, but not love. But if from all eternity, without end and without beginning, ultimate reality is a community of persons knowing and loving one another, then ultimate reality is about love relationships.

Why would a triune God create a world? If he were a unipersonal God, you might say, "Well, he created the world so he can have beings who give him worshipful love, and that would give him joy." But the triune God already had that—and he received love within himself in a far purer, more powerful form than we human beings can ever give him. So why would he create us? There's only one answer. He must have created us not to *get* joy but to *give* it. He must have created us to invite us into the dance, to say: If you glorify me, if you center your entire life on me, if you find me beautiful for who I am in myself, then you will step into the dance, which is what you are made for. You are made not just to believe in me or to be spiritual in some general way, not just to pray and get a bit of inspiration when things are tough. You are made to center everything in your life on me, to think of everything in terms of your relationship to me. To serve me unconditionally. That's where you'll find your joy. That's what the dance is about.

Are you in the dance or do you just believe God is out there somewhere? Are you in the dance or do you just pray to God every so often when you're in trouble? Are you in the dance or are you looking around for someone to orbit around you? If life is a divine dance, then you need more than anything else to be in it. That's what you're built for. *You are made to enter into a divine dance with the Trinity.*

Dancing into Battle

Immediately after Jesus's baptism, he finds himself in the wilderness. Mark writes:

> *At once the Spirit sent him out into the desert, and he was in the desert forty days, being tempted by Satan. He was with the wild animals . . .*
>
> (Mark 1:12–13)

Mark is showing us in these two lines that even though ultimate reality is a dance, we're going to experience reality as a battle. Mark weaves his account into the shared history of his readers by drawing parallels between the Hebrew Scriptures and the life of Jesus. In Genesis: The Spirit moves over the face of the waters, God speaks the world into being, humanity is created, and history is launched. What's the very next thing that happens? Satan tempts the first human beings, Adam and Eve, in the Garden of Eden.

Now here in Mark: The Spirit, the water, God speaks, a new humanity, history is altered, and immediately the pattern continues with Satan tempting Jesus in the wilderness. Mark's choice of words is pointed; he says that Jesus was "with the wild animals." At the time Mark was writing his Gospel, Christians were being thrown to wild animals. Not surprisingly, many surviving Christians were tempted to doubt their beliefs, tempted to hedge their commitment to God. But here they see Jesus, like Adam, experiencing a spectacular relationship with God and then having to contend with a threat of his own.

You see, the wilderness isn't just a random detour into trouble—*it's a battleground.* Temptation isn't impersonal—there is an actual enemy doing the tempting. Mark treats Satan as a reality, not a myth. This is certainly jarring in contemporary cultures that are skeptical of the existence of the supernatural, let alone the demonic. To us, Satan is a personification of evil left over from a pre-scientific, superstitious society. He's just a symbol now, an ironic way to deflect personal responsibility for evil. But if you believe in God, in a good personal supernatural being, it is perfectly reasonable to believe that there are evil personal supernatural beings. The Bible says that in the world, there are very real forces of evil, and these forces are tremendously complex and intelligent. Satan, the chief of these forces, is tempting us away from the dance. That's what we see with Adam in the Garden of Eden, and again with Jesus in the wilderness.

In the Garden, Adam was told, "Obey me about the tree—do not eat from the tree of the knowledge of good and evil, or you will die." Why was that the temptation? As I said earlier, God created us to orbit around him, to center our lives on him. When God says, "Don't eat, or you'll die," what is our first response? "Why?" But God doesn't explain; if you obeyed God because you understood what he was doing and how it would benefit you, then you'd actually be stationary. You'd be saying, "Okay, it makes sense. I understand why I should obey and shouldn't eat from that tree; yes, of course." God would be a means to an end, not an end in himself.

God was saying, "Because you love me, don't eat from the tree—just because I say so. Just to be in relationship with me. Obey me about the tree, and you will live." And Adam didn't. He and Eve failed their test; and the whole human race has been failing the same test ever since. Satan never stops testing us. He says, "This idea of self-giving love, where you make yourself totally vulnerable and you orbit around other people—that'll never work."

In effect, the same thing happens to Jesus in the wilderness. Though Mark doesn't tell us what Jesus's temptation is, Matthew's Gospel does. His account (in Matthew 4:1–11) basically says that Satan tempts Jesus to step out of orbit around the Father and the Spirit, and around us. To make sure everyone else centers on him, and to protect himself. And of course this temptation doesn't actually end with the literal wilderness: Throughout the remainder of Jesus's life he's assaulted by Satan, and the attack comes to a climax in another garden, the Garden of Gethsemane, the ultimate antigarden to the Garden of Eden.

We look at Adam and Eve and say, "What fools—why did they listen to Satan?" Yet we know we still have Satan's lie in our own hearts, because we're afraid of trusting God—of trusting anybody, in fact. We're stationary, because Satan tells us we should be—that's the way he fights the battle.

But God didn't leave us defenseless. God said to Jesus, "Obey me about the tree"—only this time the tree was a cross—"and you will die." And Jesus did. He has gone before you into the heart of a very real battle, to draw you into the ultimate reality of the dance. What he has enjoyed from all eternity, he has come to offer to you. And sometimes, when you're in the deepest part of the battle, when you're tempted and hurt and weak, you'll hear in the depths of your being the same words Jesus heard: "This is my beloved child—*you* are my beloved child, whom I love; with you I'm well pleased."

TWO

THE CALL

Jesus went into Galilee, proclaiming the good news of God. "The time has come," he said. "The kingdom of God is near. Repent and believe the good news!"

(Mark 1:14–15)

The first time we hear Jesus's voice in Mark's Gospel, he says, "Repent and believe the good news!" The word *repent* here means "to reverse course," or "to turn away from something." In the Bible it refers specifically to turning away from the things that Jesus hates to the things he loves. *Euangelion* in Greek, which is translated as "good news" or "gospel," combines *angelos,* the word for one announcing news, and the prefix *eu-,* which means "joyful." *Gospel* means "news that brings joy." This word had currency when Mark used it, but it wasn't religious currency. It meant history-making, life-shaping news, as opposed to just daily news.

For example, there is an ancient Roman inscription from

about the same time as Jesus and Mark. It starts: "The beginning of the gospel of Caesar Augustus." It's the story of the birth and coronation of the Roman emperor. A gospel was news of some event that changed things in a meaningful way. It could be an ascension to the throne, or it could be a victory. When Greece was invaded by Persia and the Greeks won the great battles of Marathon and Solnus, they sent heralds (or evangelists) who proclaimed the good news to the cities: "We have fought for you, we have won, and now you're no longer slaves; you're free." A gospel is an announcement of something that has happened in history, something that's been done for you that changes your status forever.

Right there you can see the difference between Christianity and all other religions, including no religion. The essence of other religions is advice; Christianity is essentially news. Other religions say, "This is what you have to do in order to connect to God forever; this is how you have to live in order to earn your way to God." But the gospel says, "This is what has been done in history. This is how Jesus lived and died to earn the way to God for you." Christianity is completely different. It's joyful news.

How do you feel when you're given good advice on how to live? Someone says, "Here's the love you ought to have, or the integrity you ought to have," and maybe they illustrate high moral standards by telling a story of some great hero. But when you hear it, how does it make you feel? Inspired, sure. But do you feel the way the listeners who heard those heralds felt when the victory was announced? Do you feel your burdens have fallen off? Do you feel as if something great has been done for you and you're not a slave anymore? Of course you don't. It weighs you down: This is how I have to live. It's not a gospel. The gospel is that God connects to you not on the basis of what you've done (or haven't done) but on the basis of what Jesus has done, in history, for you. And that makes it absolutely different from every other religion or philosophy.

Jesus says, "The kingdom of God is near. Repent and believe the good news!" What is the good news of the kingdom of God? In the book of Genesis chapters 1–2, we see that we were created to live in a world in which all relationships were whole—psychologically and socially perfect—because God was the King. But Genesis chapter 3 tells the next part of our story: that we have each chosen to be our own king. We have gone the way of self-centeredness. And self-centeredness destroys relationships. There's nothing that makes you more miserable (or less interesting) than self-absorption: How am I feeling, how am I doing, how are people treating me, am I proving myself, am I succeeding, am I failing, am I being treated justly? Self-absorption leaves us static; there's nothing more disintegrating. Why do we have wars? Class struggle? Family breakdown? Why are our relationships constantly exploding? It's the darkness of self-centeredness. When we decide to be our own center, our own king, everything falls apart: physically, socially, spiritually, and psychologically. We have left the dance. But we all long to be brought back in. This longing is embedded in the legends of many cultures, and though the stories are all different they all have a similar theme: A true king will come back, slay the dragon, kiss us and wake us out of our sleep of death, rescue us from imprisonment in the tower, lead us back into the dance. A true king will come back to put everything right and renew the entire world. The good news of the kingdom of God is this: Jesus is that true King.

I am reminded of a line from Tolkien's *Lord of the Rings*: "The hands of the king are healing hands, and thus shall the rightful king be known."[14] As a child blossoms under the authority of a wise and good parent, as a team flourishes under the direction of a skillful, brilliant coach, so when you come under the healing of the royal hands, under the kingship of Jesus, everything in your life will begin to heal. And when he comes back, everything sad will come untrue. His return will usher in the end of fear, suffering, and death.

Here again Christianity is different from other religions. Some religions say that this material world is going to end, that righteous or enlightened people will be rescued out of it and enter a kind of ethereal spiritual paradise. Other religions say that this material world is an illusion. Or perhaps you believe the earth will eventually burn up with the death of the sun and everything here will disintegrate as if it had never been. But the good news of the kingdom of God is that the material world God created is going to be renewed so that it lasts forever. When that happens you'll say, like Jewel the Unicorn at the end of *The Chronicles of Narnia*, "I've come home at last! This is my real country. . . . This is the land I've been looking for all my life."[15]

Following the King

As soon as Jesus begins to speak about the kingdom of God publicly, he selects twelve men to be his disciples—his core group of friends and followers. Mark records the first of these encounters:

> *As Jesus walked beside the Sea of Galilee, he saw Simon and his brother Andrew casting a net into the lake, for they were fishermen. "Come, follow me," Jesus said, "and I will make you fishers of men." At once they left their nets and followed him. When he had gone a little farther, he saw James son of Zebedee and his brother John in a boat, preparing their nets. Without delay he called them, and they*

left their father Zebedee in the boat with the hired men and
followed him.

(Mark 1:16–20)

Jesus immediately calls people to follow him. This is unique in Jewish tradition. Pupils chose rabbis; rabbis did not choose pupils. Those who wished to learn sought out a rabbi to say, "I want to study with you." But Mark is showing us that Jesus has a different type of authority than a regular rabbi's. You can't have a relationship with Jesus unless he calls you.

When Jesus says to Simon and Andrew, "Come, follow me," at once they leave their vocation as fishermen and follow him. When he calls James and John, they leave behind their father and friends, right there in the boat. We know from reading the rest of the Gospels that these men did fish again, and they did continue to relate to their parents. But what Jesus is saying is still disruptive. In traditional cultures you get your identity from your family. And so when Jesus says, "I want priority over your family," that's drastic. In our individualistic culture, on the other hand, saying good-bye to our parents isn't a big deal, but for Jesus to say, "I want priority over your career"—*that's* drastic. Jesus is saying, "Knowing me, loving me, resembling me, serving me must become the supreme passion of your life. Everything else comes second."

In many of our minds, such words cast the shadow of fanaticism. People in our culture are afraid of fanaticism—and for good reason, really. In this world considerable violence is being carried out by highly religious people. Even setting aside such extremism, almost everybody knows someone, personally or by reputation, who is very religious and who is also condemning, self-righteous, or even abusive. Most people today see religion as a spectrum of belief. On one end are people who say they're religious but don't really believe or live the tenets of their religion. On the other end you've got the fanatics, people who are *too* religious, who over-believe and over-live their faith. What's the solution to fanaticism? Many would say, "Well, why can't we be in the middle? Moderation in all things. Not too zealous, and not too uncommitted. Being right in the middle would be just right."

So is that the way Christianity works? Does Jesus say "Moderation in all things"? In Luke's Gospel, he says to a large crowd, "If anyone comes to me and does not hate his father and mother, his wife and children, his brothers and sisters—yes, even his own life—he cannot be my disciple" (Luke 14:26). Sound moderate? Jesus says, "If *anyone* comes to me." He doesn't say to the crowd, "Look, most of you can be moderate, but I do need a few good men and women who really want to go all the way with this discipleship." He says "anyone." There's no double standard. "If *anyone* wants to have anything to do with me, you have to hate your father and mother, wife and children, brother and sister, and even your own life, or you cannot be my disciple." That's what it means to follow Jesus.

Why does he talk about hating? In a number of other places Jesus says that you're not even allowed to hate your enemies. So what is he saying regarding one's father and mother? Jesus is not calling us to hate actively; he's calling us to hate *comparatively*. He says, "I want you to follow me so fully, so intensely, so enduringly that all other attachments in your life look like hate by comparison." If you say, "I'll obey you, Jesus, *if* my career thrives, *if* my health is good, *if* my family is together," then the thing that's on the other side of that *if* is your real master, your real goal. But Jesus will not be a means to an end; he will not be used. If he calls you to follow him, *he* must be the goal.

Does that sound like fanaticism? Not if you understand the difference between religion and the gospel. Remember what religion is: advice on how you must live to earn your way to God. Your job is to follow that advice to the best of your ability. If you follow it but don't get carried away, then you have moderation. But if you feel like you're following it faithfully and completely, you'll believe you have a connection with God because of your right living and right belief, and you'll feel superior to people who have wrong living and wrong belief. That's a slippery slope: If you feel superior to them, you stay away from them. That makes it easier to exclude them, then to hate them, and ultimately to oppress them. And there are some Christians like that—not because they've gone too far and been too committed to Jesus, but because they haven't gone far enough. They aren't as fanatically humble and sensitive, or as fanatically understanding and generous as Jesus was. Why not? *They're still treating Christianity as advice instead of good news.*

The gospel isn't advice: It's the good news that you don't need to earn your way to God; Jesus has already done it for you. And it's a gift that you receive by sheer grace—through God's thoroughly unmerited favor. If you seize that gift and keep holding on to it, then Jesus's call won't draw you into fanaticism *or* moderation. You will be passionate to make Jesus your absolute goal and priority, to orbit around him; yet when you meet somebody with a different set of priorities, a different faith, you won't assume that they're inferior to you. You'll actually seek to serve them rather than oppress them. Why? Because the gospel is not about choosing to follow advice, it's about being called to follow a King. Not just someone with the power and authority to tell you what needs to be done—but someone with the power and authority to *do* what needs to be done, and then to offer it to you as good news.

Where do we see that kind of authority? Jesus's baptism has already been attended by supernatural signs that announce his divine authority. Then we see Simon, Andrew, James, and John follow Jesus without delay—so his call itself has authority. Mark continues to build on this theme:

> *They went to Capernaum, and when the Sabbath came, Jesus went into the synagogue and began to teach. The people were amazed at his teaching, because he taught them as one who had authority, not as the teachers of the law.*
>
> (Mark 1:21–22)

Mark uses the term *authority* for the first time; the word literally means "out of the original stuff." It comes from the same root as the word *author*. Mark means that Jesus taught about life with original rather than derived authority. He didn't just clarify something that they already knew, or simply interpret the Scriptures in the way the teachers of the law did. His listeners sensed somehow that he was explaining the story of their lives *as the author*, and it left them dumbfounded. Mark then takes the theme of authority to the next level:

> *As soon as they left the synagogue, they went with James and John to the home of Simon and Andrew. Simon's mother-in-law was in bed with a fever, and they told Jesus about her. So he went to her, took her hand and helped her up. The fever left her and she began to wait on them.*
>
> (Mark 1:29–31)

The healing shows that Jesus is concerned with and king over the physical world—not just the spiritual. It is not simply a *claim* of authority (which we have in the calling of the disciples and the authoritative teaching) but is also a clear proof and exercise of Jesus's authority. He shows he has real power over sickness—just a touch of his hand and the fever is cured. And this happens over and over. Three lines later Mark records that Jesus cured whole crowds of people. A few days after that his touch cured a man with leprosy. By the middle of chapter 2 everyone is amazed, saying, "We have never seen anything like this!" The deaf hear, the blind see, and the lame walk. There are, in fact, thirty healings recorded in the Gospels, all showing us that Jesus has authority over sickness. And over the first few chapters of his Gospel, Mark goes on to stack up layer upon layer of evidence to show that Jesus's authority extends to every realm of life.

Come, follow me. Jesus is saying, "Follow me because I'm the King you've been looking for. Follow me because I have authority over everything, yet I have humbled myself for you. Because I died on the cross for you when you didn't have the right beliefs or the right behavior. Because I have brought you news, not advice. Because I'm your true love, your true life—follow me."

Following the Thread

About 150 years ago George MacDonald wrote a children's book called *The Princess and the Goblin*. Irene, the protagonist, is eight years old. She has found an attic room in her house, and every so often her fairy grandmother appears there. When Irene goes to look for her she's often not there, so one day her grandmother gives her a ring with a thread tied to it, leading to a little ball of thread. She explains that she'll keep the ball.

"But I can't see it," says Irene.

"No. The thread is too fine for you to see it. You can only feel it." With this reassurance, Irene tests the thread.

[*22*]

"Now, listen," says the grandmother, "if ever you find yourself in any danger . . . you must take off your ring and put it under the pillow of your bed. Then you must lay your forefinger . . . upon the thread, and follow the thread wherever it leads you."

"Oh, how delightful! It will lead me to you, Grandmother, I know!"

"Yes," said the grandmother, "but, remember, it may seem to you a very roundabout way indeed, and you must not doubt the thread. Of one thing you may be sure, that while you hold it, I hold it too." A few days later Irene is in bed, and goblins get into the house. She hears them snarling out in the hallway, but she has the presence of mind to take off her ring and put it under the pillow. And she begins to feel the thread, knowing that it's going to take her to her grandmother and to safety. But to her dismay, it takes her outside, and she realizes that it's taking her right toward the cave of the goblins.

Inside the cave, the thread leads her up to a great heap of stones, a dead end. "The thought struck her, that at least she could follow the thread backwards, and thus get out. . . . But the instant she tried to feel it backwards, it vanished from her touch." The grandmother's thread only worked forward, but forward it led into a heap of stones. Irene "burst into a wailing cry," but after crying she realizes that the only way to follow the thread is to tear down the wall of stones. She begins tearing it down, stone by stone. Though her fingers are soon bleeding, she pulls and pulls.

Suddenly she hears a voice. It's her friend Curdie, who has been trapped in the goblins' cave! Curdie is astounded and asks, "Why, however did you come here?"

Irene replies that her grandmother sent her, "and I think I've found out why."

After Irene has followed the thread and removed enough

rocks to create an opening, Curdie starts to climb up out of the cave—but Irene keeps going deeper into the cave. Curdie objects: "Where are you going there? That's not the way out. That's where I couldn't get out."

"I know that," says Irene. "But this is the way my thread goes, and I must follow it."[16] And indeed the thread proves trustworthy, because her grandmother is trustworthy.

When Jesus told the disciples, "We're on the way, follow me," they had no idea where he was going. They thought he was going to go from strength to strength to strength. They had no idea.

Imagine sitting down with a seven-year-old and saying to her, "I'd like you to write me an essay on what you think it's like to fall in love and be married." When you read the essay, you will say it isn't very close to the reality. A seven-year-old can't imagine what love and marriage will be like. When you start to follow Jesus, you're at least that far away. You have no idea how far you'll have to go.

Jesus says, "Follow me. I'm going to take you on a journey, and I don't want you to turn to the left or to the right. I want you to put me first; I want you to keep trusting me; to stick with me, not turn back, not give up, turn to me in all the disappointments and injustices that will happen to you. I'm going to take you places that will make you say, 'Why in the world are you taking me *there*?' Even then, I want you to trust me."

The path Jesus takes you on may look like it's taking you to one dead end after another. Nevertheless, the thread does not work in reverse. If you just obey Jesus and follow it forward, it will do its work.

MacDonald, author of *The Princess and the Goblin*, put it like this in another story: "The one secret of life and development, is not to devise and plan . . . but to do every moment's duty aright . . . and let come—not what will, for there is no such thing—but what the eternal Thought wills for each of us, has intended in each of us from the first."[17] And in yet another: "You will be dead, so long as you refuse to die."[18] That is, you will be dead so long as you refuse to die to yourself. Follow the thread. You say, "That sounds pretty hard," and you're right. How can we possibly follow the thread? It's simple but profound. Jesus himself does absolutely everything he's calling us to do. When he called James and John to leave their father in the boat, he had already left his Father's throne. "He left his Father's throne above, so free, so infinite his grace."[19] And later he's going to be ripped from his Father's presence, on the cross. It's going to look as if your thread is taking you into dead ends, places where you'll get bloody, where the only way to follow the thread looks like it could crush you. But don't try to go backward. Don't turn to the left; don't turn to the right. Jesus Christ's kingship will not crush you. He was crushed for you. He followed his thread to the cross so you can follow yours into his arms.

THREE

THE HEALING

Jesus had begun to preach and teach publicly. His words were commanding and his commands were irresistible. News of him spread like wildfire, and soon there were crowds surging forward to see him. How did Jesus react? Mark writes:

> *Very early in the morning, while it was still dark, Jesus got up, left the house and went off to a solitary place, where he prayed. Simon and his companions went to look for him, and when they found him, they exclaimed: "Everyone is looking for you!" Jesus replied, "Let us go somewhere else—to the nearby villages—so I can preach there also. That is why I have come."*
>
> (Mark 1:35–38)

Jesus got up very early to pray in a solitary place. The language indicates that this prayer was not brief and perfunctory but took hours—he was still praying by the time Simon came to get him.

When Simon told him that there were huge crowds gathered to see him, Jesus said that they should immediately leave. Though he was riding a wave of popular support, Jesus left it behind. Why? He was much more interested in the quality of the people's response to him than in the quantity of the crowd. Still the people came to him—some to hear his teaching, some to be healed, some out of curiosity, some for other reasons, but they came in great numbers:

> *A few days later, when Jesus again entered Capernaum, the people heard that he had come home. So many gathered that there was no room left, not even outside the door, and he preached the word to them. Some men came, bringing to him a paralytic, carried by four of them. Since they could not get him to Jesus because of the crowd, they made an opening in the roof above Jesus and, after digging through it, lowered the mat the paralyzed man was lying on. When Jesus saw their faith, he said to the paralytic, "Son, your sins are forgiven."*
>
> (Mark 2:1–5)

What a dramatic scene! If somebody suddenly came down through the roof as I was preaching, everything would stop—I would be speechless. What were these men so determined to get from Jesus? Well, it doesn't seem at first that Jesus understands. Jesus turns to the paralyzed man, and instead of saying "Rise up, be healed," he says, "Your sins are forgiven." If this man were from our time and place, I believe he would have said something like this: "Um, thanks, but that's not what I asked for. I'm paralyzed. I've got a more immediate problem here."

But in fact Jesus knows something the man doesn't know—that he has a much bigger problem than his physical condition.

Jesus is saying to him, "I understand your problems. I have seen your suffering. I'm going to get to that. But please realize that the main problem in a person's life is never his suffering; it's his sin." If you find Jesus's response offensive, please at least consider this: If someone says to you, "The main problem in your life is not what's happened to you, not what people have done to you; your main problem is the way you've responded to that"—ironically, that's empowering. Why? Because you can't do very much about what's happened to you or about what other people are doing—but you *can* do something about yourself. When the Bible talks about sin it is not just referring to the bad things we do. It's not just lying or lust or whatever the case may be—it is ignoring God in the world he has made; it's rebelling against him by living without reference to him. It's saying, "I will decide exactly how I live my life." And Jesus says that is our main problem.

Jesus is confronting the paralytic with his main problem by driving him deep. Jesus is saying, "By coming to me and asking for only your body to be healed, you're not going deep enough. You have underestimated the depths of your longings, the long-ings of your heart." Everyone who is paralyzed naturally wants with every fiber of his being to walk. But surely this man would have been resting all of his hopes in the possibility of walking again. In his heart he's almost surely saying, "If only I could walk again, then I would be set for life. I'd never be unhappy, I would never complain. If only I could walk, then everything would be right." And Jesus is saying, "My son, you're mistaken." That may sound harsh, but it's profoundly true. Jesus says, "When I heal your body, if that's all I do, you'll feel you'll never be unhappy again. But wait two months, four months—the euphoria won't last. The roots of the discontent of the human heart go deep."

Nobody has articulated the damage caused by that discontent

better than Cynthia Heimel, who used to write for the *Village
Voice*. She wrote an article that I've never forgotten. Over the
years she had known a number of people who were struggling
actors and actresses, working in restaurants and punching tickets
at theaters to pay their bills, and then they became famous. When
they were struggling like all of us, they said, "If only I could
make it in the business, if only I had this or that, I'd be happy."
They were like so many other people: stressed, driven, easily
upset. But when they actually got the fame they had been longing for, Heimel said, they became insufferable: unstable, angry,
and manic. Not just arrogant, as you might expect—worse than
that. They were now *unhappier* than they used to be. She said,

> I pity [celebrities]. No, I do. [Celebrities] were once
> perfectly pleasant human beings . . . but now . . . their
> wrath is awful. . . . More than any of us, they wanted
> fame. They worked, they pushed. . . . The morning
> after . . . each of them became famous, they wanted
> to take an overdose . . . because that giant thing they
> were striving for, that fame thing that was going to
> make everything okay, that was going to make their
> lives bearable, that was going to provide them with
> personal fulfillment and . . . happiness, had happened.
> And nothing changed. They were still them. The dis-
> illusionment turned them howling and insufferable.

She was sorry for them. They had the thing they had thought
would make everything okay—and it didn't. Then Heimel added
a statement that took my breath away: "I think when God wants
to play a really rotten practical joke on you, he grants your deepest wish."[20] You know what Jesus is saying to the paralyzed man?

I'm not going to play that rotten joke on you. I'm not going to just heal your body and let you think you've gotten your deepest wish.

Going Deeper

The Bible says that our real problem is that every one of us is building our identity on something besides Jesus. Whether it's to succeed in our chosen field or to have a certain relationship—or even to get up and walk—we're saying, "If I have that, if I get my deepest wish, then everything will be okay." You're looking to that thing to save you from oblivion, from disillusionment, from mediocrity. You've made that wish into your savior. You never use that term, of course—but that's what's happening. And if you never quite get it, you're angry, unhappy, empty. But if you *do* get it, you ultimately feel *more* empty, *more* unhappy. You've distorted your deepest wish by trying to make it into your savior, and now that you finally have it, it's turned on you.

Jesus says, "You see, if you have me, I will actually fulfill you, and if you fail me, I will always forgive you. I'm the only savior who can do that." But it is hard to figure that out. Many of us first start going to God, going to church, because we have problems, and we're asking God to give us a little boost over the hump so that we can get back to saving ourselves, back to pursuing our deepest wish. The problem is that we're looking to something besides Jesus as savior. Almost always when we first go to Jesus saying, "This is my deepest wish," his response is that we need to go a lot deeper than that.

C. S. Lewis put this so poetically in *The Voyage of the Dawn Treader*. There's a boy named Eustace, and everybody hates him and he hates everybody. He's selfish, he's mean, and nobody can get along with him. But he finds himself magically on a boat, the *Dawn Treader*, taking a great voyage. At one point this boat pulls in to an island, and Eustace wanders off and finds a cave. The cave proves to be filled with diamonds and rubies and gold. He thinks, "I'm rich!" And immediately, because he is who he is, he thinks that now he'll be able to pay everybody back. Anyone who has laughed at him, stepped on him, slighted him, will now get their comeuppance. Eustace then falls asleep on the pile of treasure—which he doesn't yet know is the hoard of a dragon. And because he falls asleep with greedy dragonish thoughts in his heart, when he wakes up, he's become a dragon—big, terrible, and ugly. Soon he realizes there's no way out. He can't go on the boat, he's going to be left on the island alone, he's going to be horrible all of his life. He falls into despair.

One day the great lion Aslan shows up, leads him to a clear pool of water, and tells him to undress and jump in. And suddenly Eustace realizes that "undress" means "take off the dragon skin." He begins to gnaw and claw off the scales, and he realizes that he can shed his skin. Working at it, he finally peels off this skin—but to his dismay, he finds that underneath he's got another dragon skin. He tries a second time and a third time, to no avail; the same thing still happens each time. In the end the lion says, *You're going to have to let me go deeper.* And here's how Eustace tells the story later:

> I was afraid of his claws, I can tell you, but I was pretty nearly desperate now. . . . The very first tear he made was so deep that I thought it had gone right into my heart. And when he began pulling the skin off, it hurt worse than anything I've ever felt. . . . Well, he

peeled the beastly stuff right off—just as I thought I'd done it myself the other three times, only they hadn't hurt—and there it was lying on the grass: only ever so much thicker, and darker, and more knobbly-looking than the others had been. . . . Then he caught hold of me . . . and threw me into the water. It smarted like anything but only for a moment. . . . Then I saw . . . I'd turned into a boy again.[21]

For many of us, it's hard to read that passage without weeping. Because like the paralyzed man, and like Eustace, we thought if we just got a little bit of help we could save ourselves. But we learned that Jesus wanted to take us deeper. We had to let him use his claws and go all the way to our heart and reconfigure the main thing that our heart wanted. You see, it wasn't our deepest wish itself that was the problem, just as it wasn't wrong for the paralytic to want to walk or for the celebrity to want to succeed or for Eustace to want to be loved and respected. The fact that we thought getting our deepest wish would heal us, would save us—*that was the problem*. We had to let Jesus be our Savior.

Even Deeper

When Jesus says to the paralytic, "Son, your sins are forgiven," he is doing something unexpected. So unexpected that it triggers his first clash with the religious leaders of his day:

When Jesus saw their faith, he said to the paralytic, "Son, your sins are forgiven." Now some teachers of the law were sitting there, thinking to themselves, "Why does this fellow talk like that? He's blaspheming! Who can forgive sins but God alone?" Immediately Jesus knew in his spirit that this was what they were thinking in their hearts.

(Mark 2:5–8)

Jesus can read the motives of the hearts of those around him—in this case the religious leaders. When Jesus says to the paralyzed man, "Son, your sins are forgiven," they are shocked and angry. They believe Jesus is blaspheming—showing contempt or irreverence toward God—because he claims to do something only God can do. They think to themselves: "Who can forgive sins but God alone?" They're totally right.

Let's say Tom, Dick, and Harry are talking. Tom punches Dick smack in the mouth. There's blood everywhere. Then Harry goes up to Tom and says, "Tom, I forgive you for punching Dick in the mouth. It's all right. It's over." What is Dick going to say, once he's calmed down? "Harry, you can't forgive him. Only I can forgive him. He didn't wrong you; he wronged me." You can only forgive a sin if it's against *you*. That's why, when Jesus looks at the paralyzed man and says, "Your sins are forgiven," he's actually saying, "Your sins have really been against me." The only person who can possibly say that to a human being would be their Creator. Jesus Christ, by forgiving the man, is claiming to be God Almighty. The religious leaders know it: This man is not just claiming to be a miracle worker, he is claiming to be the Lord of the universe—and they are understandably furious about it. How does Jesus respond to their thoughts?

Immediately Jesus knew in his spirit that this was what they were thinking in their hearts, and he said to them,

"Why are you thinking these things? Which is easier: to say to the paralytic, 'Your sins are forgiven,' or to say, 'Get up, take your mat and walk'? But that you may know that the Son of Man ["Son of Man" was Jesus's favorite way of referring to himself] has authority on earth to forgive sins. . . ." He said to the paralytic, "I tell you, get up, take your mat and go home." He got up, took his mat and walked out in full view of them all. This amazed everyone and they praised God, saying, "We have never seen anything like this!"

(Mark 2:8–12)

The penetrating question that Jesus asks them—"Which is easier, to say to the paralytic, 'Your sins are forgiven,' or to say, 'Get up, take up your mat, and walk'?"—has been puzzled over for twenty centuries. Once while preparing a sermon on this text I got out my Anchor Bible Commentary, which is arguably the most thorough, scholarly, and respected set of critical studies of the Bible. And when the commentator arrives at the place in Mark's Gospel where Jesus poses this question, he says, in essence, "You know, after countless pages written on this, we still have a good question before us. Which *is* easier? It's hard to say."

On the first reading, Jesus seems to be saying, "Anybody can say 'Your sins are forgiven,' but not everybody can heal. To show you therefore that I am the Lord with authority to forgive sins, I say to you, 'Pick up your mat and walk.'" The apparent implication is that it's a lot harder to heal somebody than to forgive somebody, and he is signaling his power to do the latter by performing the former. But this is such a profoundly puzzling question because it has more than one answer. Jesus is also saying: "My friends, it is going to be infinitely harder to effect the

[34]

forgiveness of sins than you can imagine. I'm not just a miracle worker; I'm the Savior. Any miracle worker can say 'Take up your mat and walk,' but only the Savior of the world can say to a human being, 'All your sins are forgiven.'"

Many biblical scholars say that here, as early as chapter 2 of Mark, the shadow of the cross falls across Jesus's path. Jesus knows what the religious leaders are thinking, so he knows that if he begins to let on that he's not just a miracle worker but also the Savior of the world, they're eventually going to kill him. If he not only heals this man but forgives his sins as well, he's taking a decisive, irreversible step down the path to his death. By taking that step, he is putting a down payment on our forgiveness.

You see, at that moment Jesus had the power to heal the man's body, just as he has the power to give you that career success, that relationship, that recognition you've been longing for. He actually has the power and authority to give each of us what we've been asking for, on the spot, no questions asked.

But Jesus knows that's not nearly deep enough. He knows that whether we're a paralyzed man lying on a mat or a struggling actor or a former struggling actor who's become a celebrity, we don't need someone who can just grant our wishes. We need someone who can go deeper than that. Someone who will use his claws, lovingly and carefully, to pierce our self-centeredness and remove the sin that enslaves us and distorts even our beautiful longings. In short, we need to be forgiven. That's the only way for our discontent to be healed. It will take more than a miracle worker or a divine genie—it will take a Savior. Jesus knows that to be our Savior he is going to have to die.

And we will discover that in the process of dealing with what we thought were our deepest wishes, Jesus has revealed an even deeper, truer one beneath—and it is for Jesus himself. He will not just have granted that true deepest wish, *he will have fulfilled it*. Jesus is not going to play the rotten practical joke of giving you your deepest wish—until he has shown you that it was for him all along.

FOUR

THE REST

Jesus claimed to be able to forgive sins, and the religious leaders called that blasphemy. But Jesus goes on to make a claim so outrageous that the leaders don't have a word for it. Jesus declares not that he has come to reform religion but that he's here to *end* religion and to replace it with himself.

> One Sabbath Jesus was going through the grain fields, and as his disciples walked along, they began to pick some heads of grain. The Pharisees said to him, "Look, why are they doing what is unlawful on the Sabbath?" He answered, "Have you never read what David did when he and his companions were hungry and in need? In the days of Abiathar the high priest, he entered the house of God and ate the consecrated bread, which is lawful only for priests to eat. And he also gave some to his companions." Then he said to them, "The Sabbath was made for man, not man for the Sabbath. So the Son of Man is Lord

*even of the Sabbath." [Remember that "Son of Man" was
Jesus's most common way of referring to himself.]*

(Mark 2:23–28)

The law of God directed that you had to rest from your work
one day in seven. That was wonderful, of course, but the religious
leaders of the day had fenced in this law with a stack of specific
regulations. There were thirty-nine types of activity that you
could not do on the Sabbath, including reaping grain, which is
what the Pharisees accused the disciples of doing. Mark goes on
to record a second incident that took place on the Sabbath day:

> *Another time [Jesus] went into the synagogue, and a man
> with a shriveled hand was there. Some of them were looking
> for a reason to accuse Jesus, so they watched him closely to see
> if he would heal him on the Sabbath. Jesus said to the man
> with the shriveled hand, "Stand up in front of everyone."
> Then Jesus asked them, "Which is lawful on the Sabbath:
> to do good or to do evil, to save life or to kill?" But they
> remained silent. He looked around at them in anger and,
> deeply distressed at their stubborn hearts, said to the man,
> "Stretch out your hand." He stretched it out, and his hand
> was completely restored. Then the Pharisees went out and
> began to plot with the Herodians how they might kill Jesus.*
>
> (Mark 3:1–6)

Why does Jesus become angry with the religious leaders?
Because the Sabbath is about restoring the diminished. It's about
replenishing the drained. It's about repairing the broken. To heal
the man's shriveled hand is to do exactly what the Sabbath is all
about. Yet because the leaders are so concerned that Sabbath regulations be observed, they don't want Jesus to heal this man—an

incredible example of missing the forest for the trees. Their hearts are as shriveled as the man's hand. They're insecure and anxious about the regulations. They're tribal, judgmental, and self-obsessed instead of caring about the man. Why? *Religion.*

Religion Versus the Gospel

Jesus shows in these encounters that there are two radically different spiritual paradigms. Imagine two people, both trying to obey the law of God, yet they operate from these two opposing paradigms. Both want to keep the Sabbath day, but in one case the obedience is a burden, an enslavement; while in the other it's a delight, a gift. How can that be? One paradigm is religion, which—as we observed before—is fundamentally *advice.* The other is the gospel of Jesus Christ, which begins and ends with *news.* These are two completely different things.

Most people in the world believe that if there is a God, you relate to God by being good. Most religions are based on that principle, though there are a million different variations on it. Some religions are what you might call nationalistic: You connect to God, they say, by coming into our people group and taking on the markers of society membership. Other religions are spiritualistic: You reach God by working your way through certain transformations of consciousness. Yet other religions are legalistic: There's a code of conduct, and if you follow it God will look upon you with favor. But they all have the same logic: If I perform, if I obey, I'm accepted. The gospel of Jesus is not only different from that but diametrically opposed to it: I'm fully accepted in Jesus Christ, and therefore I obey.

In the little town of Hopewell, Virginia, where I served as a minister for nine years, some of these distinctions became real to me for the first time. In about 1977, I preached a sermon there on "Love your neighbor as yourself," and I explained it this way: "I think God is saying, 'I want you to meet the needs of other people with all of the joy, all of the eagerness, all of the urgency, all of the ingenuity, creativity, and industry with which you meet your own needs. That's the standard. That's how I want you to live your life.'" After the service a teenage girl came up and told me that she had just been in the homecoming pageant with her best friend, and she came in last in the pageant, while her friend had won. She said, "Are you trying to tell me that the Bible says I should be as happy for her as I would have been for myself if I had won? I should be just as excited with her as if it had happened to me?"

I said, "You know, that's a pretty good application of the text. I wish I had put that in the sermon."

She looked at me and said, "Christianity is ridiculous. Who lives like that?"

We sat down to discuss it further and I reminded her, "Jesus does say, 'Love your neighbor as yourself.'"

She responded, "First of all, then, I want to know exactly who my neighbor is. It can't be everybody in the world. I could never do that. What number of square blocks around my house does the Bible's rule cover?" She went on: "And I want to know exactly what you have to do. What are the things I have to do for my neighbor?"

Do you hear the anxiety in her questions? She was not a self-righteous, morally arrogant person. But because she was not awash in the love and acceptance of God through Jesus Christ, for her the purpose of the law was to assure her that God and other people had to see her, and so treat her, as a good person. She didn't have the emotional security to handle a law that uses broad strokes to paint a life of love and obedience. She wanted to narrow it down, detail it out, button it up, so that she could feel good about herself when she had complied. We are all susceptible to this anxiety—though some have learned to hide it better than she could then.

In religion the purpose of obeying the law is to assure you that you're all right with God. As a result, when you come to the law, what you're most concerned about is detail. You want to know *exactly* what you've got to do, because you have to push all the right buttons. You won't gravitate toward seeking out the intent of the law; rather, you'll tend to write into the law all sorts of details of observance so you can assure yourself that you're obeying it. But in the life of Christians the law of God—though still binding on them—functions in a completely different way. It shows you the life of love you want to live before the God who has done so much for you. God's law takes you out of yourself; it shows you how to serve God and others instead of being absorbed with yourself. You study and obey the law of God in order to discover the kind of life you should live in order to please and resemble the one who created and redeemed you, delivering you from the consequences of sin. And you don't violate it or whittle it down to manageable proportions by adding man-made details to it.

Lord of the Sabbath

In the face of this self-righteous religious preoccupation Jesus says, "The Sabbath was made for man, not man for the Sabbath. So the Son of Man is Lord even of the Sabbath." He affirms, even celebrates, the original principle of the Sabbath—the need for rest. Yet he squashes the legalism around its observance. He dismantles the whole religious paradigm. And he does it by pointing to his identity.

Jesus could have claimed divine authority to change the Sabbath, by saying something along the lines of "I'm Lord *over* the Sabbath." But he is saying even more.

The word *Sabbath* means a deep rest, a deep peace. It's a near synonym for *shalom*—a state of wholeness and flourishing in every dimension of life. When Jesus says, "I am the Lord *of* the Sabbath," Jesus means that he *is* the Sabbath. He is the source of the deep rest we need. He has come to completely change the way we rest. The one-day-a-week rest we take is just a taste of the deep divine rest we need, and Jesus is its source.

When Jesus says, in effect, "As the Lord of the Sabbath, I can give you rest," what does that mean?

When Jesus calls you to rest, he is calling you to take time off—physical and mental time off from work on a regular basis. But there's another level of rest, a deeper level. At the end of Genesis chapter 1, the account of God's creation of the world, God is said to have rested from his work. What does that mean? Does God get tired? No, God doesn't get tired. So how could he rest? A different reason to rest is to be so satisfied with your work, so utterly satisfied, that you can leave it alone. Only when you can say about your work, "I'm so happy with it, so satisfied—it is finished!" can you walk away. When God finished creating the world, he said, "It is good." He rested.

The movie *Chariots of Fire* was based on the true story of two Olympians in the Paris competition of 1924. One of them, Eric Liddell, was a Christian, and he refused to run on the Sabbath. As a result he lost the chance for a gold medal in a race he was favored to win. At one level, taking a day off for rest is what the movie is about. But the movie added another level and contrasted Harold Abrahams with Liddell. Abrahams and Liddell were both trying very hard to win gold medals. But Abrahams was doing it out of a need to prove himself. At one point, speaking of the sprint event in which he was competing, he said, "I've got ten seconds to justify my existence."

Liddell, on the other hand, simply wanted to please the God who had already accepted him. That's why he said to his sister, "God made me fast, and when I run I feel his pleasure." Harold Abrahams was weary even when he rested, and Eric Liddell was rested even when he was exerting himself. Why? Because there's a work underneath our work that we really need rest from. It's the work of self-justification. It's the work that often leads us to take refuge in religion.

Most of us work and work trying to prove ourselves, to convince God, others, and ourselves that we're good people. That work is never over unless we rest in the gospel. At the end of his great act of creation the Lord said, "It is finished," and he could rest. On the cross at the end of his great act of redemption Jesus said, "It is finished"—and we can rest. On the cross Jesus was saying of the work underneath your work—the thing that makes you truly weary, this need to prove yourself because who you are and what you do are never good enough—that it is finished. He has lived the life you should have lived, he has died the death you should have died. If you rely on Jesus's finished work, you know that God is satisfied with you. You can be satisfied with life.

Physicians will tell you that it is not merely fitful naps that you need, but deep sleep. You can take all the vacations in the world, but if you don't have the deep rest of the soul, resting in what Jesus did on the cross, you will not truly rest. On the cross Jesus experienced the restlessness of separation from God so that we can have the deep rest of knowing that he loves us and our sins have been forgiven.

"I Am"

Jesus says he is Lord of the Sabbath. His self-awareness is startling. No other human teacher has made anything like the claims he makes. There are plenty who have said, "I'm the divine consciousness." But they think of the divinity as being in all of us, in the trees and the rocks and the human spirit. Jesus, however, understands that there is a God who is uncreated, beginningless, infinitely transcendent, who made this world, who keeps everything in the universe going, so that all the molecules, all the stars, all the solar systems are being held up by the power of this God. And Jesus says, *That's who I am.*

And he says it all the time. Jesus refers to himself throughout the Gospels in a unique manner. He says, "I am the bread of life"; "I am the light of the world"; "I am the way, and the truth, and the life"; "I am the true vine"; "I am the Good Shepherd." The use of the phrase "I Am" is significant because it is the personal name God uses for himself. It is a name so sacred that Israelites would not even utter it. And Jesus is claiming this name for himself.

Remember when Jesus healed the paralyzed man he said, "Your sins are forgiven." He was basically claiming that *all sins are against him.* Since you can only forgive sins against yourself—and sins are offenses against God—he is claiming to be God.

Every prophet, religious teacher, sage—every wise man or woman who has ever lived—has buttressed his or her statements with something like "Thus saith the Lord." *Jesus never says that.* All Jesus ever says is "Truly, truly, *I* say." Even Jesus's footnotes and sidebars—everything he says—assume that he is the uncreated, transcendent, eternal Creator of the universe.

Many people say, "Sure, I believe that Jesus is a great teacher, but I can't believe what they say about him being God." That creates a problem, because his teaching is based on his identity claim. Do you like his teachings about the Sabbath? They are based on his being Lord of the Sabbath. He is the source of the Sabbath. He is the One who created the world and then rested on the seventh day. Here is how historian N. T. Wright puts it: "How can you live with the terrifying thought that the hurricane has become human, that fire has become flesh, that life itself became life and walked in our midst? Christianity either means that, or it means nothing. It is either the most devastating disclosure of the deepest reality of the world, or it is a sham, a nonsense, a bit of deceitful playacting. Most of us, unable to cope with saying either of those things, condemn ourselves to live in the shallow world in between."[22] He's right. I believe you'll see that in the end you can't simply *like* anybody who makes claims like those of Jesus. Either he's a wicked liar or a crazy person and you should have nothing to do with him, or he is who he says he is and your whole life has to revolve around him and you have to throw everything at his feet and say, "Command me." Or do you live in that misty "world in between" that Wright says no one can live in with integrity? Do you pray to Jesus when you're in trouble, and otherwise mostly ignore him because you get busy? Either Jesus can't hear you because he's not who he says he is—or if he *is* who he says he is, he must become the still point of your turning world, the center around which your entire life revolves.

The End of Religion

At the end of this Sabbath encounter with the religious leaders Mark records a remarkable sentence that sums up one of the main themes of the New Testament, "Then the Pharisees went out and began to plot with the Herodians how they might kill Jesus."

The Herodians were the supporters of Herod, the nastiest of the corrupt kings who ruled Israel, representing the Roman occupying power and its political system. In any country that the Romans conquered, they set up rulers. And wherever the Romans went, they brought along the culture of Greece—Greek philosophy, the Greek approach to sex and the body, the Greek approach to truth. Conquered societies like Israel felt assaulted by these immoral, cosmopolitan, pagan values. In these countries there were cultural resistance movements; and in Israel that was the Pharisees. They put all their emphasis on living by the teachings of the Hebrew Scriptures and putting up big hedges around themselves to prevent contamination by the pagans. See what was going on? The Herodians were moving with the times, while the Pharisees upheld traditional virtues. The Pharisees believed their society was being overwhelmed with pluralism and paganism, and they were calling for a return to traditional moral values. These two groups had been longtime enemies of each other—but now they agree: *They have to get rid of Jesus.* These two groups were not used to cooperating, but now they do. In fact, the Pharisees, the religious people, take the lead in doing so.

That's why I say this sentence hints at one of the main themes of the New Testament. The gospel of Jesus Christ is an offense to both religion and irreligion. It can't be co-opted by either moralism or relativism.

The "traditional values" approach to life is moral conformity—the approach taken by the Pharisees. It is that you must lead a very, very good life. The progressive approach, embodied in the Herodians, is self-discovery—you have to decide what is right or wrong for you. And according to the Bible, both of these are ways of being your own savior and lord. *Both* are hostile to the message of Jesus. And not only that, both lead to self-righteousness. The moralist says, "The good people are in and the bad people are out—and of course we're the good ones." The self-discovery person says, "Oh, no, the progressive, open-minded people are in and the judgmental bigots are out—and of course we're the open-minded ones." In Western cosmopolitan culture there's an enormous amount of self-righteousness about self-righteousness. We progressive urbanites are so much better than people who think they're better than other people. We disdain those religious, moralistic types who look down on others. Do you see the irony, how the way of self-discovery leads to as much superiority and self-righteousness as religion does?

The gospel does not say, "the good are in and the bad are out," nor "the open-minded are in and the judgmental are out." The gospel says the humble are in and the proud are out. The gospel says the people who know they're *not* better, not more open-minded, not more moral than anyone else, are in, and the people who think they're on the right side of the divide are most in danger.

Jesus himself said this to the Pharisees earlier when he told them, "It is not the healthy who need a doctor, but the sick. I have not come to call the righteous, but sinners" (Mark 2:15–17). When Jesus says he is not coming for the "righteous," he does not mean that some people don't need him. The clue to what Jesus does mean is his reference to himself as a physician. You go to a doctor only when you have a health problem that you can't deal with yourself, when you feel you can't get better through self-management. What do you want from a doctor? Not just advice—but intervention. You don't want a doctor to simply say, "Yes, you sure are sick!" You want some medicine or treatment.

Jesus calls people "righteous" who are in the same position spiritually as those who won't go to a doctor. "Righteous" people believe they can "heal themselves," make themselves right with God by being good or moral. They don't feel the need for a soul-physician, someone who intervenes and does what they can't do themselves. Jesus is teaching that he has come to call sinners: those who know they are morally and spiritually unable to save themselves.

Because the Lord of the Sabbath said, "It is finished," we can rest from religion—forever.

The renowned British minister Dick Lucas once preached a sermon in which he recounted an imaginary conversation between an early Christian and her neighbor in Rome.

"Ah," the neighbor says. "I hear you are religious! Great! Religion is a good thing. Where is your temple or holy place?"

"We don't have a temple," replies the Christian. "Jesus is our temple."

"No temple? But where do your priests work and do their rituals?"

"We don't have priests to mediate the presence of God," replies the Christian. "Jesus is our priest."

"No priests? But where do you offer your sacrifices to acquire the favor of your God?"

"We don't need a sacrifice," replies the Christian. "Jesus is our sacrifice."

"What kind of religion *is* this?" sputters the pagan neighbor.

And the answer is, it's no kind of religion at all.

FIVE

THE POWER

Each part of the story Mark tells reveals a little more of who Jesus is—his power, his purpose, and his self-understanding. Mark is revealing Jesus gradually, like an expert storyteller.

But at the same time, he's also a faithful reporter. The beginning of our next story is laced with detail. In his book *Jesus and the Eyewitnesses,* biblical scholar Richard Bauckham examines the characteristics of eyewitness memory. One of the marks of an eyewitness account is "irrelevant detail."[23] Composed, fictional stories contain details that move the narrative along or convey a message that the author wants to get across. But eyewitnesses record many details simply because they remember them. It is true that fiction writers today often add small details to their stories to make them realistic. But that's not the way legends were composed in ancient times. According to Bauckham, scholars who believe the Gospel of Mark is fiction have trouble explaining why Mark, in the story we are about to read, tells us Jesus started out across the Sea of Galilee with other boats around his, or why he adds that Jesus was asleep in the boat on a cushion. These sorts of details don't advance the plot and don't develop the characters. Vincent Taylor, the prominent twentieth-century biblical scholar, said that these details were "so unnecessary to the story" and therefore have the marks of "genuine reminiscence."[24]

Mark, then, is giving us Peter's firsthand reporting. We can know that this story—which is all about the power of Jesus— really happened. Let's get into the boat and learn about this power alongside Jesus's disciples:

> *That day when evening came, he said to his disciples, "Let us go over to the other side." Leaving the crowd behind, they took him along, just as he was, in the boat. There were also other boats with him. A furious squall came up, and the waves broke over the boat, so that it was nearly swamped. Jesus was in the stern, sleeping on a cushion. The disciples woke him and said to him, "Teacher, don't you care if we drown?"*
>
> (Mark 4:35–38)

The Sea of Galilee sits seven hundred feet below sea level, and just thirty miles to the north is Mount Hermon, ninety-two hundred feet high. The cold air from the mountains continually clashes with warm air coming up from the Sea of Galilee, and as a result there are impressive thunderstorms and squalls. Professional fishermen from Galilee (like Jesus's disciples) were used to them. This storm must therefore have been an incredible one, because experienced sailors though they were, they thought they were going to die. They cried out to Jesus, "Teacher, don't you care if we drown?" How did Jesus respond? Mark records:

> *He got up, rebuked the wind and said to the waves, "Quiet! Be still!" Then the wind died down and it was*

completely calm. He said to his disciples, "Why are you so afraid? Do you still have no faith?" They were terrified and asked each other, "Who is this? Even the wind and the waves obey him!"

(Mark 4:39–41)

Jesus woke up, and two amazing things happened. The first was his words themselves, a command of utter simplicity. He didn't brace himself, roll up his sleeves, and raise a wand. There were no incantations. He said: *Quiet! Be still!* That's it. To a hurricane, Jesus simply says, *Quiet! Be still!*—just as you would talk to an unruly child.

The more astonishing thing is that the storm obeyed like a compliant child. "Then the wind died down—and it was completely calm." That sounds like redundancy until you realize that Mark is talking first about the wind and then about the water. "Completely calm" could literally be translated "dead calm." Have you ever seen water that is smooth as glass, no waves at all? You can see your face in it. When the winds stopped after Jesus's rebuke, that could have been a coincidence. But if you've ever gone on an ocean cruise or lived on the shore, you know that even when the winds stop and a storm ends, the waves keep pounding for hours afterward. Yet when Jesus said, *Quiet! Be still!* not only did the winds die down but the water instantly went dead calm.

One consensus point among the ancient cultures was that the sea was uncontrollable by any power but God. In ancient cultures and legends, the sea was a symbol of unstoppable destruction. The ocean in full fury was an ungovernable, inexorable power, and only God could control it. Did you ever hear the story of King Canute, a Danish king in the eleventh century? His fawning courtiers were flattering him excessively, and he responded, "Am I divine?" He walked to the shore and said, "Stop," and of course the ocean waves just kept coming. He was saying, "Only

God can stop the sea. I can't—I'm not God." Jesus, however, is able to exercise that power that only God has. And remember, Jesus did not conjure; he did not call on a higher authority. If you read any of the old miracle healing legends, the healers call on a higher power. They say, "In the name of _____ I say . . ." Jesus says simply *Be still* to a storm.

When Jesus was with the Pharisees on the Sabbath he said, "I am not just someone who can instruct you to take rest; I am rest *itself*." Now by his actions here Jesus is demonstrating, "I am not just someone who *has* power; I am power *itself*. Anyone and anything in the whole universe that has any power has it on loan from me."

That is a mighty claim. And if it's true, who is this and what does this mean for us? There are two options. You could argue that this world is just the result of a monumental "storm"—you're here by accident, through blind, violent forces of nature, through the big bang—and when you die, you'll turn to dust. And when the sun goes out, there won't be anyone around to remember anything that you've done, so in the end whether you're a cruel person or loving person makes no lasting difference at all. However, if Jesus is who he says he is, there's another way to look at life. If he's Lord of the storm, then no matter what shape the world is in—or your life is in—you will find Jesus provides all the healing, all the rest, all the power you could possibly want.

Unmanageable Power

Look at the emotional state of the disciples in this passage:

> *The disciples woke [Jesus] and said to him, "Teacher, don't you care if we drown?" He got up, rebuked the*

*wind and said to the waves, "Quiet! Be still!" Then the
wind died down and it was completely calm. He said to
his disciples, "Why are you so afraid? Do you still have no
faith?" They were terrified and asked each other, "Who is
this? Even the wind and the waves obey him!"*

(Mark 4:38–41)

Before Jesus calms the storm, they're afraid—but after Jesus calms the storm, they're terrified. Why? Before Jesus was awakened, Mark says, the boat was nearly swamped—it was almost full. The disciples couldn't bail fast enough; they knew the boat was just seconds from being totally filled and they would die. They woke Jesus and said, "Don't you care if we drown?" This picture goes to our hearts, because everyone who's ever tried to live a life of faith in this world has felt like this sometimes. Everything is going wrong, you're sinking, and God seems to be asleep, absent, or unaware. If you loved us, the disciples were saying, you wouldn't let us go through this. If you loved us, we wouldn't be about to sink. If you loved us, you would not be letting us endure deadly peril. Jesus calmed the storm, and then he responded to them. Did he say, I can understand how you felt? No, he asked, "Why are you so afraid?" Can you imagine what the disciples must have been thinking? What do you mean, why were we afraid? We were afraid we were going to drown. We were afraid you didn't love us, because if you loved us, you wouldn't let these things happen to us.

But Jesus's question to them has behind it this thought: Your premise is wrong. You should have known better. I *do* allow people I love to go through storms. You had no reason to panic.

If they had little reason to panic during the storm, they certainly had no reason to be afraid after it had died down. But Mark writes: "They were terrified and asked each other, 'Who is this? Even the wind and the waves obey him!'"

Why were they more terrified in the calm than they were in the storm? Because Jesus was as unmanageable as the storm itself. The storm had immense power—they couldn't control it. Jesus had infinitely more power, so they had even less control over him. But there's a huge difference. A storm doesn't love you. Nature is going to wear you down, destroy you. If you live a long time, eventually your body will give out and you'll die. And maybe it will happen sooner—through an earthquake, a fire, or some other disaster. Nature is violent and overwhelming—it's unmanageable power, and it's going to get you sooner or later. You may say, that's true, but if I go to Jesus, he's not under my control either. He lets things happen that I don't understand. He doesn't do things according to my plan, or in a way that makes sense to me. But if Jesus is God, then he's got to be great enough to have some reasons to let you go through things you can't understand. His power is unbounded, but so are his wisdom and his love. Nature is indifferent to you, but Jesus is filled with untamable love for you. If the disciples had really known that Jesus loved them, if they had really understood that he is both powerful and loving, they would not have been scared. Their premise, that if Jesus loved them he wouldn't let bad things happen to them, was wrong. He can love somebody and still let bad things happen to them, because he is God—because he knows better than they do.

If you have a God great enough and powerful enough to be mad at because he doesn't stop your suffering, you also have a God who's great enough and powerful enough to have reasons that you can't understand. You can't have it both ways. My teacher Elisabeth Elliot put it beautifully in two brief sentences: "God is God, and since he is God, he is worthy of my worship and my service. I will find rest nowhere else but in his will, and that will is necessarily infinitely, immeasurably, unspeakably beyond my largest notions of what he is up to."[25] If you're at the mercy of the storm, its power is unmanageable and it doesn't love you. The only place you're safe is in the will of God. But because he's God and you're not, the will of God is necessarily, immeasurably, unspeakably beyond your largest notions of what he is up to. Is he safe? "Of course he's not safe. Who said anything about being safe? But he's good. He's the King."[26]

Costly Power

Jesus asks the disciples, "Do you still have no faith?" That could actually be translated as "Where is your faith?" I love that way of phrasing it. By asking the question in this way, Jesus is prompting them to see that the critical factor in their faith is not its strength, but its object.

Imagine you're falling off a cliff, and sticking out of the cliff is a branch that is strong enough to hold you, but you don't know how strong it is. As you fall, you have just enough time to grab that branch. How much faith do you have to have in the branch for it to save you? Must you be totally sure that it can save you? No, of course not. You only have to have enough faith to grab the branch. That's because it's not the quality of your faith that saves you; it's the object of your faith. It doesn't matter how you feel about the branch; all that matters is the branch. And Jesus is the branch.

Let's return to George MacDonald's story *The Princess and the Goblin*, from which I quoted earlier. Curdie, a strapping young miner, has been captured by goblins and is trapped in a cave. One night little Irene, hearing goblins in her house, takes out a magic thread given to her by her fairy grandmother and starts to follow it. It takes her right down into the darkness she most dreads, but she follows it in faith, finds Curdie, and leads him out. But Curdie can't see or feel the thread. He tells Irene, "I'm very grateful that you saved my life, but I don't believe in your grandmother or the thread." Vexed, she protests, "How could I have ever saved you without the thread?" When Irene's fairy grandmother appears next, the grandmother says, "He is a good boy, Curdie, and a brave boy. Aren't you glad you have got him out?"

"Yes, Grandmother," says Irene, "but it wasn't very good of him not to believe me when I was telling him the truth." Here is how the grandmother answers: "People must believe what they can, and those who believe more must not be hard upon those who believe less. I doubt you would have believed it all yourself if you hadn't seen some of it."[27] What MacDonald is saying is extremely important and profoundly biblical. *People who believe more must not be hard on those who believe less.* Why? Because faith ultimately is not a virtue; it's a gift.

If you want to believe but can't, stop looking inside; go to Jesus and say, "Help me believe." Go to him and say, "So you're the one who gives faith! I've been trying to work it out by reasoning and thinking and meditating and going to church in hopes that a sermon will move me—I've been trying to get faith by myself. Now I see that *you're* the source of faith. Please give it to me." If you do that, you'll find that Jesus has been seeking you—he's the author of faith, the provider of faith, and the object of faith.

Something unusual happens in our response to this passage about the storm. The disciples always screwed up, and normally we respond by laughing, "They just don't get it!" But we don't feel that way in this case, do we? We sympathize. There was a storm, Jesus was asleep, they were about to sink, and they came apart. They were thinking, Jesus doesn't love us. He woke up and said, "If you knew how I love you, you would have stayed calm." That's nearly impossible, we think; we know we can't handle storms so calmly. But we have something that the disciples didn't have yet.

We have a resource that can enable us to stay calm inside no matter how the storms rage outside. Here's a clue: Mark has deliberately laid out this account using language that is parallel, almost identical, to the language of the famous Old Testament account of Jonah. Both Jesus and Jonah were in a boat, and both boats were overtaken by a storm—the descriptions of the storms are almost identical. Both Jesus and Jonah were asleep. In both stories the sailors woke up the sleeper and said, "We're going to die." And in both cases, there was a miraculous divine intervention and the sea was calmed. Further, in both stories the sailors then became even more terrified than they were before the storm was calmed. Two almost identical stories—with just one difference. In the midst of the storm, Jonah said to the sailors, in effect: "There's only one thing to do. If I perish, you survive. If I die, you will live" (Jonah 1:12). And they threw him into the sea. Which doesn't happen in Mark's story. Or does it? I think Mark is showing that the stories aren't actually different when you stand back a bit and look at them with the rest of the story of Jesus in view. In Matthew's Gospel, Jesus says, "One greater than Jonah is here," and he's referring to himself: *I'm the true Jonah.* He meant this: Someday I'm going to calm all storms, still all waves. I'm going to destroy destruction, break brokenness, kill death. How can he do that? He can do it only because when he was on the cross he was thrown—willingly, like Jonah—into the ultimate storm, under the ultimate waves, the waves of sin and death. Jesus was thrown into the only storm that can actually sink us—the storm of eternal justice, of what we owe for our wrongdoing. That storm wasn't calmed—not until it swept him away.

If the sight of Jesus bowing his head into that ultimate storm is burned into the core of your being, you will never say, "God, don't you care?" And if you know that he did not abandon you in that ultimate storm, what makes you think he would abandon you in the much smaller storms you're experiencing right now? And, someday, of course, he will return and still all storms for eternity.

If you let that penetrate to the very center of your being, you will know he loves you. You will know he cares. And then you will have the power to handle anything in life with poise.

> When through the deep waters I call you to go,
> The rivers of woe shall not overflow;
> For I will be with you, your troubles to bless,
> And sanctify to you your deepest distress.
>
> The soul that on Jesus has leaned for repose,
> I will not, I will not desert to its foes;
> That soul, though all hell should endeavor to shake,
> I'll never, no never, no never forsake.[28]

SIX

THE WAITING

Grant that we may follow the example of Jesus's patience." That is what Thomas Cranmer, the author of the original *Book of Common Prayer*, wrote as a prayer to be used on Palm Sunday—the Sunday before Easter. What does he mean by patience? Patience is love for the long haul; it is bearing up under difficult circumstances, without giving up or giving in to bitterness. Patience means working when gratification is delayed. It means taking what life offers—even if it means suffering—without lashing out. And when you're in a situation that you're troubled over or when there's a delay or pressure on you or something's not happening that you want to happen, there's always a temptation to come to the end of your patience. You may well have lost your patience before you're even aware of it.

Cranmer's prayer is particularly poignant because it is prayed the week before Easter, the time when we remember Jesus's sacrificial death on the cross. Jesus displayed patience not just in the way he faced his execution and his enemies. He also displayed remarkable patience with his disciples—think of his patience with them in the storm—and with the people he met throughout his life.

Mark records the meeting of Jesus with a religious leader, a ruler in the synagogue, named Jairus. He would have been a man of great devotion to God, morally respectable, as well as a figure of wealth and social prominence. Mark writes:

> *When Jesus had again crossed over by boat to the other side of the lake, a large crowd gathered around him while he was by the lake. Then one of the synagogue rulers, named Jairus, came there. Seeing Jesus, he fell at his feet. . . .*
>
> (Mark 5:21–22)

Here is a man of authority and standing, yet he falls at the feet of a Galilean carpenter. That's pretty unusual, isn't it? He must be desperate. So what's the problem? Mark tells us:

> *Seeing Jesus, he fell at his feet and pleaded earnestly with him, "My little daughter is dying. Please come and put your hands on her so that she will be healed and live." So Jesus went with him.*
>
> (Mark 5:22–24)

His little girl is as good as dead. That's the language he uses: She is going to die unless Jesus comes. So you can imagine Jairus's excitement when he realizes there's hope for his dying daughter, yet his insides must be churning with fear that he and Jesus will be too late. So Jesus, Jairus, and the disciples hurry toward Jairus's home, and they're followed by a crowd of people eager to see another miracle:

> *A large crowd followed and pressed around him. And a woman was there who had been subject to bleeding for*

twelve years. She had suffered a great deal under the care of many doctors and had spent all she had, yet instead of getting better she grew worse.

(Mark 5:24–26)

It is interesting that the text says that "she had suffered a great deal under the care of many doctors . . . yet instead . . . grew worse." In other words, she had not simply been suffering from her disease, but also from the cures. She had exhausted all her finances, and all the medical options:

When she heard about Jesus, she came up behind him in the crowd and touched his cloak, because she thought, "If I just touch his clothes, I will be healed." Immediately her bleeding stopped and she felt in her body that she was freed from her suffering. At once Jesus realized that power had gone out from him.

(Mark 5:27–30)

The crowd is pressing in on Jesus, this woman touches him and is healed, and we read that Jesus realized power had gone out from him. This is the first time the Greek word *dunamis*, "power," from which we get the word *dynamite*, is used in the book of Mark. Jesus has a sensation of weakness, of draining, and he knows that there's been a healing. He has lost power so she could gain it. He stops the entourage, the emergency procession, and he turns around and says, "I need to find out who touched me":

He turned around in the crowd and asked, "Who touched my clothes?" "You see the people crowding against you,"

his disciples answered, "and yet you can ask, 'Who touched
me?'" But Jesus kept looking around to see who had done it.
Then the woman, knowing what had happened to her,
came and fell at his feet and, trembling with fear, told
him the whole truth.

(Mark 5:30–33)

When Jesus finds the person who was healed by tapping into his power, he stops and has her tell "the whole truth," the whole story of what happened.

Imagine Jairus's anxiety during all of this; the disciples' irritation; Jesus's patience and composure. This woman with a chronic condition is getting attention instead of the little girl who has an acute condition. Jesus chooses to stop and talk with the woman who has just been healed. This makes no sense. It is absolutely irrational. In fact, it's worse than that: It's malpractice. If these two were in the same emergency room, any doctor who treated the woman first and let the little girl die would be sued. And Jesus is behaving like such a reckless doctor. Jairus and the disciples must be thinking, "What are you doing? Don't you understand the situation? Hurry, or it will be too late. The little girl needs help from you now, Jesus. Hurry, Jesus, hurry."

But Jesus will not be hurried. As he's standing there and talking with the woman, the thing that Jairus feared all along happens:

While Jesus was still speaking, some men came from the
house of Jairus, the synagogue ruler. "Your daughter is
dead," they said. "Why bother the teacher anymore?"

(Mark 5:35)

Imagine how Jairus feels about Jesus at that moment. But Jesus looks at him calmly and,

> *Ignoring what they said, Jesus told the synagogue ruler, "Don't be afraid; just believe."*
>
> (Mark 5:36)

In essence, Jesus says to Jairus, *Trust me. Be patient. There's no need to hurry.* Every culture has a different sense of time. This becomes glaringly evident in cross-cultural encounters and events. Picture a wedding where the groom is from a culture where being fifteen or thirty minutes late is okay, while the bride is from a culture that frowns on any lateness whatsoever. She and her bridesmaids are ready for the wedding but the groom isn't there and it's fifteen past the hour. On the left side of the sanctuary there's hand-wringing and worried glances. On the right side, everybody's calm. Timing is relative. And everybody has a sense of "*this* is the right time but not *this*."

God's sense of timing will confound ours, no matter what culture we're from. His grace rarely operates according to our schedule. When Jesus looks at Jairus and says "Trust me, be patient," in effect he is looking over Jairus's head at all of us and saying, "Remember how when I calmed the storm I showed you that my grace and love are compatible with going through storms, though you may not think so? Well, now I'm telling you that my grace and love are compatible with what seem to you to be unconscionable delays." It's not "I will not be hurried even though I love you"; it's "I will not be hurried *because* I love you. I know what I'm doing. And if you try to impose your understanding of schedule and timing on me, you will struggle to feel loved by me." Jesus will not be hurried, and as a result, we often feel exactly like Jairus, impatient because he's delaying irrationally, unconscionably, inordinately.

What We Really Need

But precisely because of the delay both Jairus and the woman get far more than they asked for. Be aware that when you go to Jesus for help, you will both give to and get from him far more than you bargained for. Be patient, because the deal often doesn't work out the way you expected. Take Jairus. He came to Jesus to cure his dying daughter, but he got far more than that. Let's go to the climax of this story. The plot has thickened again: Even though the little girl's dead, Jesus looks at the father and says, "I'm coming anyway." They proceed:

> *He did not let anyone follow him except Peter, James, and John, the brother of James. When they came to the home of the synagogue ruler, Jesus saw a commotion, with people crying and wailing loudly. He went in and said to them, "Why all this commotion and wailing? The child is not dead but asleep." But they laughed at him.*
>
> (Mark 5:37–40)

When they eventually arrive at Jairus's home everyone is in mourning for the dead girl. So of course they laugh when Jesus says she's asleep. They know a dead child when they see one. The story continues:

> *After he put them all out, he took the child's father and mother and the disciples who were with him, and went in where the child was. He took her by the hand and said to*

[64]

*her, "Talitha koum!" (which means, "Little girl, I say to
you, get up!"). Immediately the girl stood up and walked
around (she was twelve years old). At this they were completely astonished.*

(Mark 5:40–42)

Of course they were astonished. Jairus came to Jesus for a
fever cure, not for a resurrection. When you go to Jesus for help,
you get from him far more than you had in mind.

But when you go to Jesus for help, you also end up giving to
him far more than you expected to give. Jairus came thinking
he would have to trust Jesus just enough to get home, hoping
that somehow the child wouldn't die before he arrived. But Jesus
demanded far more from him: After Jairus's daughter had died,
because of the apparent malpractice of the Great Physician, Jesus
looked right into his eyes and said, "Trust me." Now, that was a
test of faith far beyond anything Jairus had anticipated.

Or take the sick woman. She came to Jesus for healing. But
she wanted to just touch and run. She wanted to say, "I'm better,
I'm out of here"—simple as that. Jesus wouldn't have it. Jesus
forced her to go public. Keep in mind that this was very threaten-
ing for her. She had been coping with a blood flow, which made
her ceremonially unclean. Because of this, to touch a rabbi in
public would break a great taboo. And therefore Jesus's request
that she identify herself was a very frightening thing.

Why did Jesus insist that she go public? She needed it. You see,
she had a somewhat superstitious understanding of Jesus's power.
She thought it was the touch that could heal her. She thought his
power was manageable. And Jesus made her identify herself so he
could say, "Oh, no, it was faith that healed you." Let's go now to
the climax of her story:

*Then the woman, knowing what had happened to her,
came and fell at his feet and, trembling with fear, told
him the whole truth. He said to her, "Daughter, your
faith has healed you. Go in peace and be freed from your
suffering."*

(Mark 5:33–34)

Jesus is saying to her, "Your faith is what healed you and now that you know that, you are in a life-transforming relationship with me." There's all the difference in the world between being a superstitious person who gets a bodily healing, and a life-transformed follower of Jesus for all eternity.

If you go to Jesus, he may ask of you far more than you originally planned to give, but he can give to you infinitely more than you dared ask or think.

What We Really Need to Know

As far as Jairus and the disciples are concerned, it's malpractice for Jesus to let a little girl die while he deals with a woman with a chronic condition. But we who have read to the end of the story know something that they did not. We know that for Jesus to raise a girl from the dead or to cure a fever was no different—that he has power over death. We also know that Jesus had an opportunity to take a superstitious woman who has received a bodily healing and turn her into a life-transformed follower. Jairus and the disciples couldn't see that either. They had no idea.

It seemed to Jairus and the disciples that Jesus was delaying for no good reason, but they didn't have all the facts. And so often, if God seems to be unconscionably delaying his grace and committing malpractice in our life, it's because there is some crucial information that we don't yet have, some essential variable that's unavailable to us. If I could sit down with you and listen to the story of your life, it may well be that I would join you in saying, "I can't understand why God isn't coming through. I don't know why he is delaying." Believe me, I know how you feel, so I want to be sensitive in the way I put this. But when I look at the delays of God in my own life, I realize that a great deal of my consternation has been rooted in arrogance. I complain to Jesus, "Okay, you're the eternal Son of God, you've lived for all eternity, you created the universe. But why would you know any better than I do how my life should be going?" Jacques Ellul, in his classic *The Technological Society,* argues that in modern Western society we have been taught that nearly everything in life is there to be manipulated for our own ends.[29] It has been common for many people to act in that way no matter what their time or place, but Ellul believes modern Western culture makes this condition even worse. We're not God, but we have such delusions of grandeur that our self-righteousness and arrogance sometimes have to be knocked out of our heart by God's delays.

Right now, is God delaying something in your life? Are you ready to give up? Are you impatient with him? There may be a crucial factor that you just don't have access to. The answer, as with Jairus, is to trust Jesus.

How We Really Know It

Do you think it is odd that when Jesus arrives at Jairus's house he says that the girl is just sleeping? The parallel accounts of this story in Matthew's and Luke's Gospels make it clear that Jesus understands she's dead. She's not just *mostly* dead; she's *all* dead. Then why does he make that reference to sleep?

The answer is in what Jesus does next. Remember, Jesus sits down beside the girl, takes her by the hand, and says two things to her. The first is *talitha*. Literally, it means "little girl," but that does not get across the sense of what he's saying. This is a pet name, a diminutive term of endearment. Since this is a diminutive that a mother would use with a little girl, probably the best translation is "honey." The second thing Jesus says to her is *koum*, which means "arise." Not "be resurrected"; it just means "get up." Jesus is doing exactly what this child's parents might do on a sunny morning. He sits down, takes her hand, and says, "Honey, it's time to get up." And she does. Jesus is facing death, the most implacable, inexorable enemy of the human race and such is his power that he holds this child by the hand and gently lifts her right up through it. "Honey, get up." Jesus is saying by his actions, "If I have you by the hand, death itself is nothing but sleep."

But Jesus's words and actions are not just powerful; they are loving too. When you were little, if your parent had you by the hand you felt everything was okay. You were wrong, of course. There are bad parents, and even the best parents are imperfect. Even the best parents can slip up, even the best parents make wrong choices. But Jesus is the ultimate Parent who has you by the hand and will bring you through the darkest night. The Lord of the universe, the One who danced the stars into place, takes you by the hand and says, "Honey, it's time to get up."

Why would we want to hurry somebody this powerful and this loving, who treats us this tenderly? Why would we be impatient with somebody like this? Jesus holds us by the hand and brings us through the greatest darkness. What enables him to do that? In his letter to the church in Corinth, 2 Corinthians 13:4, the apostle Paul says Christ was crucified in weakness so that we can live in God's power. Christ became weak so that we can be strong. There's nothing more frightening for a little child than to lose the hand of the parent in a crowd or in the dark, but that is nothing compared with Jesus's own loss. He lost his Father's hand on the cross. He went into the tomb so we can be raised out of it. He lost hold of his Father's hand so we could know that once he has us by the hand, he will never, ever forsake us.

That's the reason, by the way, that Thomas Cranmer's Palm Sunday prayer reads as it does. The complete prayer actually says, "Grant that we may both follow the example of his patience, and also be made partakers of his resurrection." Jesus Christ knew the only way to the crown was through the cross. The only way to resurrection was through death. So his healing of the sick woman was another foreshadowing of the cross. He lost power so she could gain strength. But on the cross he lost his very life, so we could live forever. The only way for Jesus to give us this power and life was to go through weakness and death.

Are you trying to hurry Jesus? Are you impatient with the waiting? Let him take you by the hand, let him do what he wants to do. He loves you completely. He knows what he's doing. Soon it will be time to wake up.

Let us be conformed to his patience, that we might be made partakers of the resurrection.

SEVEN

THE STAIN

Jesus's conflict with the religious leaders of his day did not abate. Mark relates an incident in which Jesus and these leaders were disagreeing about the cleanliness laws, the dietary laws, the regulations that had to do with ritual purity. It would be easy to assume that the controversy over such laws is arcane, maybe of some antiquarian interest but surely not relevant to us today. But actually it takes up matters that are profoundly relevant for human life in any culture, any century. Here's what happened:

> *The Pharisees and some of the teachers of the law who had come from Jerusalem gathered around Jesus and saw some of his disciples eating food with hands that were "unclean," that is, unwashed. (The Pharisees and all the Jews do not eat unless they give their hands a ceremonial washing, holding to the tradition of the elders. When they come from the marketplace they do not eat unless they wash. And they observe many other traditions, such as the*

washing of cups, pitchers and, kettles.) So the Pharisees and teachers of the law asked Jesus, "Why don't your disciples live according to the tradition of the elders instead of eating their food with 'unclean' hands?"

(Mark 7:1–5)

According to the cleanliness laws, if you touched a dead animal or human being, if you had an infectious skin disease like boils or rashes or sores, if you came into contact with mildew (on your clothes, articles in your home, or your house itself), if you had any kind of bodily discharge, or if you ate meat from an animal designated as unclean, you were considered ritually impure, defiled, stained, unclean. That meant you couldn't enter the temple—and therefore you couldn't worship God with the community. Such strenuous boundaries seem harsh to us, but if you think about it, they are not as odd as they sound. Over the centuries, people have fasted from food during seasons of prayer. Why? It's an aid for developing spiritual hunger for God. Also, people of various faiths kneel for prayer. Isn't that rather uncomfortable? It's an aid for developing spiritual humility. So the washings and efforts to stay clean and free from dirt and disease that were used by religious people in Jesus's day were a kind of visual aid that enabled them to recognize that they were spiritually and morally unclean and couldn't enter the presence of God unless there was some kind of spiritual purification.

If you're going to meet up with somebody who is particularly important to you—for that big date or important job interview—you wash, you brush your teeth, you comb your hair. What are you doing? Getting rid of the uncleanness, of course. You don't want a speck or stain on you. You don't want to smell bad. The cleanliness laws were the same idea. Spiritually, morally, unless you're clean, you can't be in the presence of a perfect and holy God.

Jesus couldn't have agreed more with the religious leaders of his day about the fact that we are unclean before God, unfit for the presence of God. But he disagreed with them about the source of the uncleanness, and about how to address it. Mark records:

> *Jesus called the crowd to him and said, "Listen to me, everyone, and understand this. Nothing outside a man can make him 'unclean' by going into him. Rather, it is what comes out of a man that makes him 'unclean.'"*
>
> (Mark 7:14–16)

According to Jesus, in our natural state we're unfit for the presence of God. Most modern people have a problem with this idea. Many would say, "Okay, ancients found the world a scary place because they didn't understand the way nature worked, and so they created myths to help them explain the world. They wanted to feel more in control of their destinies. They conjured up moral absolutes and wrathful deities that had to be appeased. When anything went wrong, it had to be that the gods were unhappy. Therefore ancient people were constantly ridden with shame and guilt." Nowadays, they would go on, we've moved on from moral absolutes. Nobody knows what's right and wrong for certain, nobody knows about God for certain. We all have to decide for ourselves and not be held to others' standards. Besides, we believe in human rights and the dignity of the individual. We don't see the individual as unclean, defiled, evil. We think human nature is basically good.

That's what we often say today. If there is a God, we don't believe he is a transcendently holy deity before whom we stand guilty and condemned.

And yet we still wrestle with profound feelings of guilt and shame. Where do they come from?

The Stain

One of the great writers of the twentieth century, the brilliant and bizarre Franz Kafka, explores this problem in his book *The Trial*. In the beginning of the story, Joseph K. is having a normal life, but then he is arrested and taken into custody. Nobody tells him what he did wrong. *What am I arrested for? What have I been accused of?* He is not told. He goes from one prison cell to another to another, and then to a hearing, then another. Nobody ever explains. Everybody is hard, implacable, unsympathetic. They say, "You have to talk to my supervisor, I've got my orders." He continues from hearing to hearing, custody to custody. Nobody ever tells him what's wrong. Joseph K. puzzles over his whole life. *Maybe it was for that. Have I been arrested for that? I did that. That doesn't seem like it would have been bad enough, but maybe this happened . . .* He never does find out. And in the end, one of the wardens stabs him and he dies.

In one of his diaries Kafka says something that many have taken to be the theme of *The Trial*: "The state in which we find ourselves today is sinful, quite independent of guilt."[30] In other words, we live in a world now where we don't believe in judgment, we don't believe in sin, and yet we still feel that there's something wrong with us. Kafka was really on to something. Though we've abandoned the ancient categories, we still have a profound, inescapable sense that if we were examined we'd be rejected. We have a deep sense that we've got to hide our true self or at least control what people know about us. Secretly we feel that we aren't acceptable, that we have to prove to ourselves and other people that we're worthy, lovable, valuable.

Why do we work so very hard, always saying, "If I can just get to this level, then I can relax"? And we never do relax once we get there—we just work and work. What is driving us? Why is it that some of us can never allow ourselves to disappoint anybody? We have no boundaries, no matter what people ask of us, how much they exploit us, trample on us, because to disappoint somebody is a form of death. Why does that possibility bother us so much? Where are all the self-doubts coming from? Why are we so afraid of commitment? Kafka is saying, "You don't believe in sin, you don't believe in judgment, you don't believe in guilt—and yet you know somehow you're unclean." You may psychologize it: I have a complex, my parents didn't love me enough, I'm a victim, I have self-esteem issues. But there's no escaping the fact that we all have a sense we're unclean.

Outside-In Cleansing

Jesus shows us why we can't shake that sense of uncleanness. The story continues:

> After [Jesus] had left the crowd and entered the house, his disciples asked him about this parable. "Are you so dull?" he asked. "Don't you see that nothing that enters a man from the outside can make him 'unclean'? For it doesn't go into his heart but into his stomach, and then out of his body." (In saying this, Jesus declared all foods "clean.")
>
> (Mark 7:17–19)

Jesus's language is quite graphic here: Whether you eat clean or unclean food it goes into the mouth, down to the stomach, and then (literally) out into the latrine. It never gets to the heart. Nothing that comes in from the outside makes us unclean.

> He went on: "What comes out of a man is what makes him 'unclean.' For from within, out of men's hearts, come evil thoughts, sexual immorality, theft, murder,

*adultery, greed, malice, deceit, lewdness, envy, slander,
arrogance and folly. All these evils come from inside and
make a man 'unclean.'"*

(Mark 7:20–23)

What's really wrong with the world? Why can the world be such
a miserable place? Why is there so much strife between nations,
races, tribes, classes? Why do relationships tend to fray and fall
apart? Jesus is saying: *We are what's wrong.* It's what comes out
from the inside. It's the self-centeredness of the human heart.
It's sin. In fact, these evils that come from the heart make us so
unclean that Jesus later tells the disciples:

*"If your hand causes you to sin, cut it off. It is better
for you to enter life maimed than with two hands to go
into hell, where the fire never goes out. And if your foot
causes you to sin, cut it off. It is better for you to enter life
crippled than to have two feet and be thrown into hell.
And if your eye causes you to sin, pluck it out. It is better
for you to enter the kingdom of God with one eye than to
have two eyes and be thrown into hell, where 'their worm
does not die, and the fire is not quenched.'"*

(Mark 9:43–48)

Sinful behavior (the reference to hand and foot) and sinful
desires (the reference to the eye) are like a fire that has broken
out in your living room. Let's say a cushion on your couch has
ignited. You cannot just sit there and say, "Well, the whole house
isn't burning—it's just a cushion." If you don't do something
immediately and decisively about the cushion, the whole house
will be engulfed. Fire is never satisfied. It can't be allowed to
smolder; it can't be confined to a corner. It will overtake you

eventually. Sin is the same way: It never stays in its place. It always leads to separation from God, which results in intense suffering, first in this life and then in the next. The Bible calls that hell. That's why Jesus uses the drastic image of amputation. There can be no compromises. We must do anything we can to avoid it: If our foot causes us to sin, we should cut it off. If it's our eye, we should cut it out.

But Jesus has just pointed out that our biggest problem, the thing that makes us most unclean, is not our foot or our eye; it's our heart. If the problem were the foot or the eye, although the solution would be drastic, it would be possible to deal with it. But we can't cut out our heart. No matter what we do, or how hard we try, external solutions don't deal with the soul. Outside-in will never work, because most of what causes our problems works from the inside out. We will never shake that sense that we are unclean.

As Aleksandr Solzhenitsyn said, "The line between good and evil passes not through states, nor between classes, nor between political parties either—but right through every human heart—and through all human hearts."[31] Time after time the Bible shows us that the world is not divided into the good guys and the bad guys. There may be "better guys" and "worse guys," but no clear division can be made between the good and the bad. Given our sin and self-centeredness, we all have a part in what makes the world a miserable, broken place.

Yet we're all *still* trying to address that sense of uncleanness through external measures, trying to do something that Jesus says is basically impossible. Let me give some examples. One example is religion itself: If I stay away from dirty movies and profane activities and bad people, if I pray and read my Bible, if I try really hard to be good, then God will see that I'm worthy and come in and heal my heart. The problem is that, as Jesus said, that model doesn't stick. You never feel you're good enough. Though you're praying and trying your very best to be good, your heart doesn't change. You're never filled with love and joy and security. You're actually more anxious, because you never know if you're living up. When something goes wrong in your life, you'll immediately be thrown into doubt: "I thought I was living a good enough life. Why did God let this happen?" You never find out. Religion doesn't get rid of the self-justification, the self-centeredness, the self-absorption, at all. It doesn't really strengthen and change the heart. It's outside-in.

Politics tends to work outside-in as well. Right after World War II a great many British political intellectuals found their entire worldview shattered by what had happened during the war. In 1952, just before he died, C. M. Joad, a socialist philosopher who had been an atheist, published a book, *The Recovery of Belief*, in which he tells of coming back to belief in God. He said, "It was because we rejected the doctrine of original sin that we on the Left were always being so disappointed; disappointed by the refusal of people to be reasonable . . . by the behavior of nations and politicians . . . above all, by the recurrent fact of war."[32] Both the behavior of the people and of the leaders were inexplicable to his circle of intellectuals, Joad argues, because they didn't believe in sin. Lord David Cecil said this after the Holocaust: "The jargon of the philosophy of progress taught us to think that the savage and primitive state of man is behind us. . . . But barbarism is not behind us, it is [within] us."[33]

Dorothy Sayers, a British writer and poet who lived at the same time, said that World War II was a terrible blow to the educated class of England, who had "an optimistic belief in the civilizing influence of progress and enlightenment." These were the people who found "the appalling outbursts of bestial ferocity in the totalitarian states, the obstinate selfishness and stupid greed of capitalist society, not . . . merely shocking and alarming. For them, these things are the utter negation of everything in which they have believed. It is as though the bottom had dropped out of their universe."[34]

In her book *Creed or Chaos?* Sayers said that over the previous century and more, politics had operated on the following basis: What was wrong with human society was not in the human heart. It lay in social structures, in a lack of education. It was a lack of applying what we know through science. Therefore, if we could just fill those gaps, human society would achieve greatness. But modern history is littered with disillusioned people who thought capitalism would make us better or socialism would make us better. The sins of the human heart just express themselves differently in each of these systems. Politics is another outside-in approach that does not change the heart.

Then there is the world of popular culture. Christina Kelly was a very successful editor of young women's magazines; over a period of several years she was on the staff of *Elle Girl*, *YM*, *Jane*, and *Sassy*. Some years back she wrote a confessional piece in which she asked:

> Why do we crave celebrities? Here's my theory. To be human is to feel inconsequential. So we worship celebrities and we seek to look like them. All the great things they have done we identify with in order to escape our own inconsequential lives. But it's so dumb. With this stream of perfectly airbrushed, implanted, liposuctioned stars, you would have to be an absolute powerhouse of self-esteem already not to feel totally inferior before them. So we worship them because we feel inconsequential, but doing it makes us feel even worse. We make them stars, but then their fame makes

us feel insignificant. I am part of this whole process as an editor. No wonder I feel soiled at the end of the day.[35]

That is so Kafkaesque. *To be human is to feel inconsequential.* Every one of us has at some time or other felt this kind of inexplicable sense of inconsequentiality, that we're unclean, that we need to prove ourselves. Popular culture says to us, "Aha, here's a way to be clean: Be pretty. Have flawless skin. Change your look. Get thin. Look like a celebrity." But Christina Kelly says the celebrities themselves are incredibly unsuccessful in dealing with their sense of inconsequentiality through their beauty, while the rest of us feel worse because we can't even come close to them. Outside-in doesn't work.

Maybe you're saying, "Religion's not my thing, nor politics, and I'm not into popular culture." Just to show you that we're *all* trying to cleanse ourselves from the outside in and it doesn't work, let me turn briefly to Christian ministry itself. You'll see that no one is immune. Why do people go into a life of ministry? Noble motivations, right? Some years ago I read this line in a book for ministry students by Charles Spurgeon: "Don't preach the gospel in order to save your soul." I was in my twenties at the time, and I remember thinking, "What kind of idiot would try to save his soul by preaching the gospel?" But after a few years in the ministry, you start to realize that if your church does well and grows and people like you, you feel disproportionately good—and if your church doesn't do well and people don't really like you, you feel disproportionately devastated. You're working outside in. You had assumed, "If people like me and say, 'Oh, how much you help me,' then God will like me and I will like myself, and then that sense of inconsequentiality, that sense of uncleanness, will go away." But it doesn't. Many years ago I was reading a critical study that rendered Romans 1:17 in the following way: "He who through faith is righteous shall live," and I almost heard a voice saying, "Yes, and he who through preaching is righteous shall die every Sunday."[36]

You see, we're all trying to cleanse ourselves, or to cover our uncleanness by compensatory good deeds. But it will not work. The prophet Jeremiah puts this very vividly: " 'Although you wash yourself with soda and use an abundance of soap, the stain of your guilt is still before me,' declares the Sovereign LORD" (Jeremiah 2:22). Outside-in cleansing cannot deal with the problem of the human heart.

Inside-Out Cleansing

Unlike Matthew, Luke, and John, Mark almost never makes editorial comments or interpretations in his book. So when Mark does make an interpretive comment, it's really significant. And he makes one in this story: "In saying this, Jesus declared all foods 'clean.' "

It doesn't read, "Jesus said all foods were clean." If it did, then maybe the meaning would be, "Jesus says you don't need to worry so much about these foods, everything is all right, go ahead, eat them." Jesus would be saying that the cleanliness laws were an outdated idea, and let's get beyond them. He would be giving an authoritative opinion on the subject.

But that's not what happened. It reads, "Jesus *declared*." Jesus *pronounced*. Greek experts and scholars agree: Jesus is saying, *As of now I make these foods clean.* I called the world into being; I called the storm to a halt; I called a girl back from death. And now I call all foods clean. In order to understand the magnitude of this, you have to remember that Jesus has an incredibly high regard for the Word of God. He considers it binding, even on himself. In Matthew's Gospel he says that not a jot or a tittle— that is, not a letter—will pass away from the Word of God until it is all fulfilled.[37] Now, the cleanliness laws are a part of the Word of God. Jesus would never look at any part of it and say, "I'm abolishing this; we've gotten beyond this now." So what he is saying here is that *the cleanliness laws have been fulfilled*—that their purpose, to get you to move toward spiritual purification, has been carried out. The reason you don't have to follow them as you once did is that they've been fulfilled. What an incredible thing to say.

How could that be?

Years ago my wife Kathy and I heard a sermon preached by Ray Dillard, an Old Testament professor at Westminster Seminary and friend of ours who has since passed away. He wept through most of the sermon, which was based on Zechariah 3. Zechariah is one of the prophetic books in the Old Testament, and in the first line of chapter 3, Zechariah, in a vision, is transported into the center of the temple. He says this: "Then [the Lord] showed me Joshua, the high priest standing before the angel of the LORD."

The temple had three parts: the outer court, the inner court, and the holy of holies. The holy of holies was completely sur-rounded by a thick veil. Inside was the ark of the covenant, on top of it was the mercy seat, and the *shekinah* glory of God, the very presence and face of God, appeared over the mercy seat. It was a dangerous place. In Leviticus 16, God says, "If you come near the mercy seat, put a lot of incense and smoke up in the air, because I appear in the cloud over the mercy seat and I don't want you to die." Only one person on one day of the year was allowed to go into the holy of holies: the high priest of Israel on the Day of Atonement, Yom Kippur. Zechariah, then, was expe-riencing a vision from the center of the temple, inside the holy of holies, and he saw Joshua the high priest standing before the Lord on Yom Kippur.

Ray Dillard, preaching his sermon, then drew on his scholarship and spoke in great detail about the enormous amount of preparation that took place for the Day of Atonement. A week beforehand, the high priest was put into seclusion—taken away from his home and into a place where he was completely alone. Why? So he wouldn't accidentally touch or eat anything unclean. Clean food was brought to him, and he'd wash his body and prepare his heart. The night before the Day of Atonement he didn't go to bed; he stayed up all night praying and reading God's Word to purify his soul. Then on Yom Kippur he bathed head to toe and dressed in pure, unstained white linen. Then he went into the holy of holies and offered an animal sacrifice to God to atone, or pay the penalty for, his own sins. After that he came out and bathed completely again, and new white linen was put on him, and he went in again, this time sacrificing for the sins of the priests. But that's not all. He would come out a third time, and he bathed again from head to toe and they dressed him in brand-new pure linen, and he went into the holy of holies and atoned for the sins of all the people.

Did you know that this was all done in public? The temple was crowded, and those in attendance watched closely. There was a thin screen, and he bathed behind it. But the people were present: They saw him bathe, dress, go in, come back out. He was their representative before God, and they were there cheering him on. They were very concerned to make sure that everything was done properly and with purity, because he represented them before God. When the high priest went before God there wasn't a speck on him; he was as pure as pure can be. Only if you understand that do you realize why the next lines of the prophecy in Zechariah 3 were so shocking: Zechariah saw Joshua the high priest standing before the presence of God in the holy of holies—but Joshua's garments were covered in excrement. He was absolutely defiled. Zechariah couldn't believe his eyes. Ray said the key interpretive question is: How could that have happened? There's no way that the Israelites would ever have allowed the high priest to appear before God like that. Ray's answer was this: God was giving Zechariah a prophetic vision so that he could see us the way that God sees us. In spite of all our efforts to be pure, to be good, to be moral, to cleanse ourselves, God sees our hearts, and our hearts are full of filth.

All of our morality, all of our good works, don't really get to the heart, and Zechariah suddenly realized that no matter what we do we're unfit for the presence of God. But just as he was about to despair, he heard: " 'Take off his filthy clothes.' Then he said to Joshua, 'See, I have taken away your sin, and I will put rich garments on you. . . . Listen, . . . I am going to bring my servant, the Branch, . . . and I will remove the sin of this land in a single day' " (Zechariah 3:4 and 8–9). Zechariah probably couldn't believe his ears. He must have thought, "Wait a minute, for years we've been doing the sacrifices, obeying the cleanliness laws. We can never get the sin off ourselves!" But God was saying, "Zechariah, this is a prophecy. Someday the sacrifices will be over, the cleanliness laws will be fulfilled."

How can that be? Ray Dillard closed the sermon like this: Centuries later another Joshua showed up, another Yeshua. Jesus, Yeshua, Joshua—it's the same name in Aramaic, Greek, and Hebrew. Another Joshua showed up, and he staged his own Day of Atonement. One week beforehand, Jesus began to prepare. And the night before, he didn't go to sleep—but what happened to Jesus was exactly the reverse of what happened to Joshua the high priest, because instead of cheering him on, nearly everyone he loved betrayed, abandoned, or denied him. And when he stood before God, instead of receiving words of encouragement, the Father forsook him. Instead of being clothed in rich garments, he was stripped of the only garment he had, he was beaten, and he was killed naked. He was bathed too, Ray told us—in human spit.

Why? "God made him who had no sin to be sin for us, so that in him we might become the righteousness of God" (2 Corinthians 5:21). God clothed Jesus in our sin. He took our penalty, our punishment so that we, like Joshua, the high priest, can get what Revelation 19:7–8 pictures: "Let us rejoice and be glad. . . . Fine linen, bright and clean, is given [to us] to wear." Pure linen—perfectly clean—without stain or blemish. Hebrews 13 says Jesus was crucified outside the gate where bodies are burned—the garbage heap, a place of absolute uncleanliness—so that we can be made clean. Through Jesus Christ, at infinite cost to himself, God has clothed us in costly clean garments. It cost him his blood. And it is the only thing that can deal with the problem of your heart.

Are you living with a specific failure in your past that you feel guilty about and that you have spent your life trying to make up for? Or perhaps you are more like Kafka: not particularly religious, not especially immoral, yet you're fighting that sense of your own inconsequentiality. You might be doing it through religion or politics or beauty. You might even be doing it through Christian ministry. Doing, doing, doing from the outside in. *It won't work.*

> Cast your deadly "doing" down—
> Down at Jesus' feet;
> Stand in Him, in Him alone,
> Gloriously complete.[38]

EIGHT

THE APPROACH

How do you approach God? How do you connect with him? Most of us can think of two options. There is the ancient understanding: God is a bloodthirsty tyrant who needs to be constantly appeased by good behavior if not outright sacrifice. And there's the modern understanding of God: He's a spiritual force we can access anytime we want, no questions asked. But Mark tells us a story showing us that approaching God might mean something else entirely:

> Jesus left that place and went to the vicinity of Tyre. He entered a house and did not want anyone to know it; yet he could not keep his presence secret. In fact, as soon as she heard about him, a woman whose little daughter was possessed by an evil spirit came and fell at his feet. The woman was a Greek, born in Syrian Phoenicia. She begged Jesus to drive the demon out of her daughter.
>
> (Mark 7:24–26)

The story begins with the mysterious statement that Jesus went to the vicinity of Tyre and did not want anyone to know it. What was going on? Well, Jesus had been spending all of his time ministering in Jewish provinces, and that ministry was drawing overwhelming crowds, and he was exhausted. So Jesus left the Jewish provinces and went into a Gentile territory, Tyre, in order to get some rest.

But it doesn't work. A woman hears of his arrival and makes her way boldly to Jesus. Though she's a Syrophoenician, because of Tyre's proximity to Judea she would have known the Jewish customs. She knows that she has none of the religious, moral, and cultural credentials necessary to approach a Jewish rabbi—she is a Phoenician, a Gentile, a pagan, a woman, and her daughter has an unclean spirit. She knows that in every way, according to the standards of the day, she is unclean and therefore disqualified to approach any devout Jew, let alone a rabbi. But she doesn't care. She enters the house without an invitation, falls down and begins begging Jesus to exorcise a demon from her daughter. The verb *beg* here is a present progressive—she *keeps on begging*. Nothing and no one can stop her. In Matthew's Gospel chapter 15, the parallel account, the disciples urge Jesus to send her away. But she's pleading with Jesus—she won't take no for an answer.

You know why she has this burst of boldness, don't you? There are cowards, there are regular people, there are heroes, and then there are parents. Parents are not really on the spectrum from cowardice to courage, because if your child is in jeopardy, you simply do what it takes to save her. It doesn't matter whether you're normally timid or brazen—your personality is irrelevant. You don't think twice; you do what it takes. So it's not all that surprising that this desperate mother is willing to push past all the barriers.

So what is Jesus's response to this woman as she is down on the floor begging? The story continues:

> *She begged Jesus to drive the demon out of her daughter. "First let the children eat all they want," he told her, "for it is not right to take the children's bread and toss it to their dogs."*
>
> (Mark 7:26–27)

On the surface, this appears to be an insult. We are a canine-loving society, but in New Testament times most dogs were scavengers—wild, dirty, uncouth in every way. Their society was *not* canine-loving, and to call someone a dog was a terrible insult. In Jesus's day the Jews often called the Gentiles dogs because they were "unclean." Is what Jesus says to her just an insult, then? No, it's a parable. The word *parable* means "metaphor" or "likeness," and that's what this is. One key to understanding it is the very unusual word Jesus uses for "dogs" here. He uses a diminutive form, a word that really means "puppies." Remember, the woman is a mother. Jesus is saying to her, "You know how families eat: First the children eat at the table, and afterward their pets eat too. It is not right to violate that order. The puppies must not eat food from the table before the children do." If we go to Matthew's account of this incident, he gives us a slightly longer version of Jesus's answer in which Jesus explains his meaning: "I was sent only to the lost sheep of Israel." Jesus concentrated his ministry on Israel, for all sorts of reasons. He was sent to show Israel that he was the fulfillment of all Scripture's promises, the fulfillment of all the prophets, priests, and kings, the fulfillment of the temple. But after he was resurrected, he immediately said to the disciples, "Go to all the nations." His words, then, are not the insult they appear to be. What he's saying to the Syrophoenician woman is, "Please understand, there's an order here. I'm going to Israel first, then the Gentiles (the other nations) later." However, this mother comes back at him with an astounding reply:

> "Yes, Lord," she replied, "but even the dogs under the table eat the children's crumbs." Then he told her, "For such a reply, you may go; the demon has left your daughter." She went home and found her child lying on the bed, and the demon gone.
>
> (Mark 7:28–30)

In other words, she says, *Yes, Lord, but the puppies eat from that table too, and I'm here for mine.* Jesus has told her a parable in which he has given her a combination of challenge and offer, and she gets it. She responds to the challenge: "Okay, I understand. I am not from Israel, I do not worship the God that the Israelites worship. Therefore, I don't have a place at the table. I accept that."

Isn't this amazing? She doesn't take offense; she doesn't stand on her rights. She says, "All right. I may not have a place at the table—but there's more than enough on that table for everyone in the world, and I need mine now." She is wrestling with Jesus in the most respectful way and she will not take no for an answer. I love what this woman is doing.

In Western cultures we don't have anything like this kind of assertiveness. We only have assertion of our rights. We do not know how to contend unless we're standing up for our rights, standing on our dignity and our goodness and saying, "This is what I'm owed." But this woman is not doing that at all. This is rightless assertiveness, something we know little about. She's not saying, "Lord, give me what I deserve on the basis of my goodness." She's saying, "Give me what I *don't* deserve on the basis of *your* goodness—and I need it now."

Accepting the Challenge

Do you see how remarkable it is that she recognizes and accepts both the challenge *and* the offer hidden within it?

A good translation of Jesus's rabbinical reply to her would be "Such an answer!" Some of the translations have Jesus saying "Wonderful answer, incredible answer." And so her plea is answered and her daughter is healed. In his study of Mark, biblical scholar James Edwards puts it wonderfully:

> She appears to understand the purpose of Israel's Messiah better than Israel does. Her pluck and persistence are a testimony to her trust in the sufficiency and surplus of Jesus: his provision for the disciples and Israel will be abundant enough to provide for one such as herself. . . . What an irony! Jesus seeks desperately to teach his chosen disciples—yet they are dull and uncomprehending; Jesus is reluctant to even speak to a walk-on pagan woman—and after one sentence she understands his mission and receives his unambiguous commendation. . . . How is this possible? The answer is that the woman is the first person in Mark to hear and understand a parable of Jesus. . . . That she answers Jesus from "within" the parable, that is, in the terms by which Jesus addressed her, indicates that she is the first person in the Gospel to *hear* the word of Jesus to her.[39]

Similarly, Martin Luther was amazed and moved by this encounter, because he saw the gospel in it. This woman saw the gospel—that you're more wicked than you ever believed, but at the same time more loved and accepted than you ever dared to hope. On the one hand, she is not too proud to accept what the gospel says about her unworthiness. She accepts Jesus's challenge. She doesn't get her back up and say, "How dare you use a racial epithet about me? I don't have to stand for this!" Can you hear yourself saying that? But on the other hand, neither does this woman insult God by being too discouraged to take up his offer. See, there are two ways to fail to let Jesus be your Savior. One is by being too proud, having a superiority complex—not to accept his challenge. But the other is through an inferiority complex—being so self-absorbed that you say, "I'm just so awful that God couldn't love me." That is, not to accept his offer. John Newton, a minister, once wrote a letter to a man who was very depressed. Take note of what he said:

> You say you feel overwhelmed with guilt and a sense of unworthiness? Well, indeed you cannot be too aware of the evils inside of yourself, but you may be, indeed you are, improperly controlled and affected by them. You say it is hard to understand how a holy God could accept such an awful person as yourself. You then express not only a low opinion of yourself, which is right, but also too low an opinion of the person, work, and promises of the Redeemer, which is wrong. You complain about sin, but when I look at your complaints, they are so full of self-righteousness, unbelief, pride, and impatience that they are little better than the worst evils you complain of.[40]

It is just as much a rejection of the love of God to refuse to seek him, to refuse to come after his mercy, to refuse to accept it, to refuse to be content with it, as to say "I'm too good for it."

One of the great prayers of the English language is the prayer of approach to the Lord's Supper, written by Thomas Cranmer, in the first *Book of Common Prayer*; it's based on this story in Mark, and over the centuries millions of people have prayed it:

> We do not presume to come to this your table, merciful Lord, trusting in our own righteousness, but in your manifold and great mercies. We are not worthy so much as to gather up the crumbs under your table, but you are the same Lord whose property is always to have mercy.

Every time anyone has ever prayed that prayer, Cranmer has been inviting them to step into this woman's shoes and approach Jesus boldly, with rightless assertiveness. To take up both the offer and challenge of God's infinite mercy.

Accepting the Gift

The Syrophoenician woman approached Jesus boldly, under her own initiative. She knew what she wanted and was determined to get it. Sometimes, however, our approach to Jesus takes an altogether different trajectory; sometimes our first encounter with him feels almost accidental. But either way, Jesus knows us and gives us what we need. As soon as Jesus leaves Tyre, Mark records this story:

> *Then Jesus left the vicinity of Tyre and went through Sidon, down to the Sea of Galilee and into the region of the Decapolis. There some people brought to him a man who was deaf and could hardly talk, and they begged*

him to place his hand on the man. After he took him aside, away from the crowd, Jesus put his fingers into the man's ears. Then he spit and touched the man's tongue. He looked up to heaven and with a deep sigh said to him, "Ephphatha!" (which means, "Be opened!"). At this, the man's ears were opened, his tongue was loosened and he began to speak plainly. Jesus commanded them not to tell anyone. But the more he did so, the more they kept talking about it. People were overwhelmed with amazement. "He has done everything well," they said. "He even makes the deaf hear and the mute speak."

(Mark 7:31–37)

Jesus does a whole series of things with the deaf and mute man: He takes him away from the crowd; he points to his ears; he then touches his own tongue, takes his own saliva, and puts it on the man's tongue; he looks up, sighs, and says, "Be opened!" You might say, "Well, Jesus is doing the rituals of a miracle worker." Actually, no: Remember that in every miracle we have witnessed, from calming the storm to bringing Jairus's daughter back to life to the healing of the Syrophoenician woman's daughter, there was no arm-waving, no incantation, no mumbo-jumbo. Jesus obviously does not need to perform a ritual in order to summon his power. Which means Jesus is doing all this not because he needs it but because the man needs it.

Jesus's response to the woman's request to heal her daughter is enigmatic, cryptic, even astringent. With the deaf-mute he's melt-in-your-mouth sweet. In John's Gospel chapter 11, after Lazarus has died, he comes to be with Martha and Mary, the sisters. Martha says, "Lord, if you had been here, my brother would not have died," and Jesus rebukes her. Then Mary comes up and says, "Lord, if you had been here, my brother would not have died," and Jesus just weeps with her. Same words—by no means the same response. Why? Because Jesus always gives you what you need, and he knows better than you what that is. He's the Wonderful Counselor.

Jesus deeply identifies with this man. All the touching of his ears, touching his mouth—it's sign language. Jesus is saying, "Let's go over here; don't be afraid, I'm going to do something about that; now let's look to God." He comes into the man's cognitive world and uses terms—nonverbal speech—that he can understand. Notice how he takes him away from the crowd. Why does he do that—wouldn't he want everyone to see? Well, imagine this man as he grew up. He's always been a spectacle. He's deaf, and therefore he can't produce proper speech. Just imagine the way people made fun of him all his life. Jesus knows this, and refuses to make a spectacle of him now. He is identifying with him emotionally.

But there's a deeper identification yet, because at one point Jesus utters a *deep* sigh. A better translation might be "he moaned." A moan is an expression of pain. Why would Jesus be in pain? Maybe it's because he has emotionally connected with the man and his alienation and isolation. That's true, but he's about to heal him. Why isn't Jesus grinning at the man saying, "Wait till you see what I'm going to do for you"? Because an even deeper identification is going on: There is a cost for Jesus's healing this man. Mark deliberately signals this with the word he uses for "deaf and could hardly talk." A single Greek word, *moglilalos*, is used there and no other place in the Bible except Isaiah 35:5. It's a very rare word, and Mark would have no reason to use it unless he wanted us to cross-reference what's happening here with Isaiah 35. The prophet Isaiah says this about the Messiah: "'Be strong, do not fear; your God will come . . . with divine retribution . . . to save you.' Then will the eyes of the blind be open and the ears of the deaf unstopped. Then will the lame leap like a deer, and the mute tongue shout for joy" (Isaiah 35:4–6). Mark is saying: Do you see the blind opening their eyes? Do you see the deaf hearing, do you hear the mute tongue shouting for joy? God has come, just as Isaiah 35 promised; God has come to save you. Jesus Christ is God come to save us. Jesus is the King.

There's something else Mark wants his readers to think about. Isaiah says the Messiah will come to save us "with divine retribution." But Jesus isn't smiting people. He's not taking out his sword. He's not taking power; he's giving it away. He's not taking over the world; he's serving it. Where's the divine retribution? And the answer is, he didn't come to *bring* divine retribution; he came to *bear* it. On the cross, Jesus would identify with us totally. On the cross, the Child of God was thrown away, cast away from the table without a crumb, so that those of us who are not children of God could be adopted and brought in. Put another way, the Child had to become a dog so that we could become sons and daughters at the table.

And because Jesus identified like that with us, now we know why we can approach him. The Son became a dog so that we dogs could be brought to the table; he became mute so that our tongues can be loosed to call him King. Don't be too isolated to think you are beyond healing. Don't be too proud to accept what the gospel says about your unworthiness. Don't be too despondent to accept what the gospel says about how loved you are.

NINE

THE TURN

Chapter 8 of Mark's Gospel is a pivotal chapter. It's the climax of the first act, in which the disciples finally begin to see the true identity of the one they have been following. In it Jesus says two things: *I'm a King, but a King going to a cross*; and *If you want to follow me, you've got to come to the cross too.* This is how Mark tells the story:

> *Jesus and his disciples went on to the villages around Caesarea Philippi. On the way he asked them, "Who do people say I am?" They replied, "Some say John the Baptist; others say Elijah; and still others, one of the prophets." "But what about you?" he asked. "Who do you say I am?" Peter answered, "You are the Christ." Jesus warned them not to tell anyone about him.*
>
> (Mark 8:27–30)

Here at last Peter begins to get the answer to the big question, "Who is Jesus?" He proposes to Jesus, "You are the Christ." Peter is using a word that literally means "anointed one." Kings were traditionally anointed with oil as a kind of coronation, but the word *Christos* had come to mean *the* Anointed One, the Messiah, the King to end all kings, the King who's going to put everything right. *You are the Messiah,* Peter says. Jesus accepts the title—but then immediately turns around and begins to say things they find appalling and shocking. "Yes, I'm the King," he says, "but I'm not anything like the king you were expecting":

> He then began to teach them that the Son of Man must suffer many things and be rejected by the elders, chief priests and teachers of the law, and that he must be killed and after three days rise again. He spoke plainly about this, and Peter took him aside and began to rebuke him.
>
> (Mark 8:31–32)

Jesus's first important statement here is "The Son of Man must suffer." When we hear Jesus referring to himself as the *Son of Man,* we assume he's saying he is human—but this title means much more than that. In the prophecies of Daniel there's a reference to "one like a son of man" (Daniel 7:13–14), a divine messianic figure who comes with the angels to put everything right.

But Jesus says the Son of Man "must *suffer* . . ." Never before this moment had anyone in Israel connected suffering with the Messiah. Of course there are many prophecies in the Old Testament about a mysterious Servant of the Lord who suffers (for example the prophet Isaiah in chapters 43, 44, and 53), but nobody before Jesus had ever associated those texts with the hope of the Messiah. The notion that the Messiah would suffer made no sense at all, because the Messiah was supposed to defeat evil and injustice and make everything right in the world. How could he defeat evil by suffering and dying? That seemed ridiculous, impossible.

By using the word *must*, Jesus is also indicating that he is planning to die—that he is doing it voluntarily. He is not merely predicting it will happen. This is what probably offends Peter the most. It is one thing for Jesus to say, "I will fight and will be defeated," and another to say, "This is why I came; I intend to die!" That is totally inexplicable to Peter.

That's why the minute Jesus says this, Peter begins to "rebuke" him. This is the verb used elsewhere for what Jesus does to demons. This means Peter is condemning Jesus in the strongest possible language. Why is Peter so undone, that he would turn on Jesus like this right after identifying him as the Messiah? From his mother's knee Peter had always been told that when the Messiah came he would defeat evil and injustice by ascending the throne. But here is Jesus saying, "Yes, I'm the Messiah, the King, but I came not to live but to die. I'm not here to take power but to lose it; I'm here not to rule but to serve. And that's how I'm going to defeat evil and put everything right."

Jesus didn't just say that the Son of Man would suffer; he said that the Son of Man *must* suffer. This word is so crucial that it's employed twice: "the Son of Man must suffer many things and . . . he must be killed." The word *must* modifies and controls the whole sentence, and that means that everything in this list is a necessity. Jesus must suffer, must be rejected, must be killed, must be resurrected. This is one of the most significant words in the story of the world, and it's a scary word. What Jesus said was not just "I've come to die" but "I *have to* die. It's absolutely necessary that I die. The world can't be renewed, and nor can your life, unless I die." Why would it be absolutely necessary for Jesus to die?

A Personal Necessity

Some years ago a theologian named William Vanstone wrote a book, now out of print, that included an interesting chapter called "The Phenomenology of Love."[41] All human beings, he says— even people who from childhood were deprived of love—know the difference between false and true love, fake and authentic love.

Here's the difference, Vanstone says. In false love your aim is to use the other person to fulfill your happiness. Your love is conditional: You give it only as long as the person is affirming you and meeting your needs. And it's nonvulnerable: You hold back so that you can cut your losses if necessary. But in true love, your aim is to spend yourself and use yourself for the happiness of the other, because your greatest joy is that person's joy. Therefore your affection is unconditional: You give it regardless of whether your loved one is meeting your needs. And it's radically vulnerable: You spend everything, hold nothing back, give it all away. Then Vanstone says, surprisingly, that our real problem is that nobody is actually fully capable of giving true love. We want it desperately, but we can't give it. He doesn't say we can't give any kind of real love at all, but he's saying that nobody is fully capable of true love. All of our love is somewhat fake. How so? Because we need to be loved like we need air and water. We can't live without love. That means there's a certain mercenary quality to our relationships. We look for people whose love would really affirm us. We invest our love only where we know we'll get a good return. Of course when we do that, our love is conditional and nonvulnerable, because we're not loving the person simply for himself or herself; we're loving the person partly for the love we're getting.

Obviously there are healthy people and unhealthy people; some are more able to love than others. But at the core Vanstone is right: Nobody can give anyone else the kind or amount of love they're starved for. In the end we're all alike, groping for true love and incapable of fully giving it. What we need is someone to love us who doesn't need us at all. Someone who loves us radically, unconditionally, vulnerably. Someone who loves us just for our sake. If we received that kind of love, that would so assure us of our value, it would so fill us up, that maybe we could start to give love like that too. Who can give love with no need? Jesus. Remember the dance of the Trinity—the Father, the Son, and the Spirit have been knowing and loving one another perfectly for all eternity. Within himself, God has forever had all the love, all the fulfillment, and all the joy that he could possibly want. He has all the love within himself that the whole human race lacks. And the only way we're going to get any more is from him. A young woman in our church wrote this note to a friend:

> A major [issue] in my life has been people-pleasing. I needed approval, to be liked, admired, accepted. But for the first time I was able to see how important it was that I identified with Christ—his love has enabled me to set up emotional boundaries with people that I never could before. This has enabled me to love my friends and family for who they are and not seek more from them, because I can find whatever is lacking in Christ. It's been a huge relief to finally feel free enough to love people and know that in Christ, I am safe and protected and that protecting myself or standing up for myself is actually a good thing.

Do you see how the security of Jesus's love enables her to *need* less, and to love more? True love, love without neediness, is generative; it is the only kind that makes more of itself as it goes along.

Why did God create us and later redeem us at great cost even though he doesn't need us? He did it because he loves us. His love is perfect love, radically vulnerable love. And when you begin to get it, when you begin to experience it, the fakery and manipulativeness of your own love starts to wash away, and you've got the patience and security to reach out and start giving a truer love to other people.

A Legal Necessity

Yet we don't need Jesus's sacrifice only personally; we also need it legally. What do I mean by that? When someone really wrongs you, a debt is established that has to be paid by someone. It can happen at an economic level. What if a friend of yours accidentally smashes a lamp in your apartment? One of two things can happen as a result. Either you can make him pay—"That will be $100, please"—or you can say, "I forgive you, that's okay." But in the latter case what happens to that $100? You have to pay it yourself, or you have to lose $100 worth of light and get used to a darker room. Either your friend pays the cost for what was done or you absorb the cost. This works at levels beyond the economic, too. When someone robs you of an opportunity, robs you of happiness, of reputation, or takes away something else that you'll never get back, that creates a sense of debt. Justice has been violated—this person owes you. Once you sense that debt, again there are only two things you can do.

One thing you can do is to try to make that person pay: You can try to destroy *their* opportunities or ruin *their* reputation; you can hope they suffer, or you can actually see to it. But there's a big problem with that. As you're making them pay off the debt, as you're making them suffer because of what they did to you, you're becoming like them. You're becoming harder, colder; you're becoming like the perpetrator. Evil wins. What else can you do? The alternative is to forgive. But there's nothing easy about real forgiveness. When you want to harbor vengeful thoughts, when you want so much to carry out vengeful actions but you refuse them in an effort to forgive, it hurts. When you refrain, when you forgive, it's agony. Why? Instead of making the other person suffer, you're absorbing the cost yourself. You aren't trying to get your reputation back by tearing their reputation down. You are forgiving them and it is costing you. That's what forgiveness is. True forgiveness always entails suffering.

So the debt of wrong doesn't vanish: Either they pay or you pay. But here's the irony. Only if you pay that price of forgiveness, only if you absorb the debt, is there any chance of righting the wrong. If you confront somebody with what they've done wrong while you've got vengeance in your heart, they probably won't listen to you. They'll sense that you are not seeking justice but revenge, and they'll reject anything you say. You'll just perpetuate the cycle of retaliation, retaliation, retaliation. Only if you have refrained from vengeance and paid the cost of forgiveness will you have any hope of getting them to listen to you, of seeing their own error. And even if they do not listen to you at first, your forgiveness breaks the cycle of further reprisals. If we know that forgiveness always entails suffering for the forgiver and that the only hope of rectifying and righting wrongs comes by paying the cost of suffering, then it should not surprise us when God says, "The only way I can forgive the sins of the human race is to suffer—either you will have to pay the penalty for sin or I will." Sin always entails a penalty. Guilt can't be dealt with unless someone pays.

The only way God can pardon us and not judge us is to go to the cross and absorb it into himself. "I *must* suffer," Jesus said.

A Cosmic Necessity

Jesus *had to* die, then. But couldn't he have just thrown himself off a cliff? Or waited for the inevitable demise of his human body? No.

Jesus's death had to be a violent one. The writer of Hebrews says that "without the shedding of blood, there is no remission of sin" (Hebrews 9:22). This is not a magical view of blood. Rather, the term *blood* in the Bible means a life given or taken before its natural end. A life given or taken is the most extreme gift or price that can be paid in this world.[42] Only by giving his life could Jesus have made the greatest possible payment for the debt of sin. Jesus's death was not only a payment, however; it was also a demonstration. The scholar James Edwards writes:

> The prediction of Jesus' passion conceals a great irony, for the suffering and death of the Son of Man will not come, as we would expect, at the hands of a godless and wicked people . . . rather at the hands of "the elders, chief priests, and teachers of the law". . . . Jesus will not be lynched by an enraged mob or beaten to death in a criminal act. He will be arrested with official warrants, and tried and executed by the world's envy of jurisprudence—the Jewish Sanhedrin and the *principia iuris Romanorum*.[43]

The Jewish chief priests, teachers of the law, and, of course, the Roman rulers should have been standing up for justice but instead conspired to commit an act of injustice by condemning Jesus to death. The cross reveals the systems of the world to be corrupt, serving power and oppression instead of justice and truth. In condemning Jesus, the world was condemning itself. Jesus's death demonstrates not only the bankruptcy of the world, but it also reveals the character of God and of his kingdom. Jesus's death was not a failure. By submitting to death as penalty, he broke its hold on him and on us.[44]

When Jesus went to the cross and died for our sins, he won through losing; he achieved our forgiveness on the cross by turning the values of the world on their head. He did not "fight fire with fire." He didn't come and raise an army in order to put down the latest corrupt regime. He didn't take power; he gave it up—and yet he triumphed. On the cross, then, the world's misuse and glorification of power was exposed for what it is and defeated. The spell of the world's systems was broken.

The corrupt powers of this world have many tools to make people afraid, the worst one being death. When you know that a civil power or some other power can kill you, you're scared, and they can use your fear to control you. But since Jesus died and rose again from the dead, if you can find a way to approach Jesus and cling to him, you know that death, the worst thing that can possibly happen to you, is now the best thing. *Honey, get up.* Death will put you in God's arms and make you all you hoped to be. And when death loses its sting, when death no longer has power over you because of what Jesus did on the cross, then you will be living a life of love and not a life of fear.

A New Kind of King

Jesus says, "I'm a King, but not like any king you ever imagined. I'm a king who must die." Yet he does not stop there. Mark writes:

> *Then he called the crowd to him along with his disciples and said: "If anyone would come after me, he must deny himself and take up his cross and follow me. For whoever wants to save his life will lose it, but whoever loses his life for me and for the gospel will save it. What good is it for a man to gain the whole world, yet forfeit his soul? Or what can a man give in exchange for his soul? If anyone is ashamed of me and my words in this adulterous and*

sinful generation, the Son of Man will be ashamed of him
when he comes in his Father's glory with the holy angels."
And he said to them, "I tell you the truth, some who are
standing here will not taste death before they see the king-
dom of God come with power."

(Mark 8:34–9:1)

Jesus is saying, "Since I am a King on a cross, if you want to follow me *you* must go to a cross." What does it mean to take up our cross? What does it mean to lose our life for the gospel in order to save it?

The deliberately chosen Greek word for "life" here is *psyche*, from which we get our word *psychology*. It denotes your identity, your personality, your selfhood—what makes you distinct. Jesus is not saying, "I want you to lose your sense of being an individual self." That's a teaching of Eastern philosophy, and if he meant that, he would have said, "You must lose yourself to lose yourself." Jesus is saying, "Don't build your identity on gaining things in the world." His exact words are, "What good is it for a man to gain the whole world, yet forfeit his soul?"

Every culture points to certain things and says, "If you gain those, if you acquire or achieve those, then you'll have a self, you'll know you're valuable." Traditional cultures would say you're nobody unless you gain the respectability and legacy of family and children. In individualistic cultures it's different; the culture says you're nobody unless you gain a fulfilling career that brings money, reputation, and status. Regardless of such differences, though, every culture says identity is performance-based, achievement-based.

And Jesus says that will never work. If you gain the whole world, he says, it won't be big enough or bright enough to cover up the stain of inconsequentiality. No matter how many of these

[104]

things you gain, it's never enough to make you sure of who you are. If you're building your identity on "somebody loves me," or if you're building your identity on "I've got a good career," and anything goes wrong with that relationship or that job, you fall apart. You feel like you don't have a self.

Are you beginning to see how radical Jesus is? It's not a matter of saying, "I've been a failure, I've been immoral, so now I'm going to go to church and become a moral, decent person. Then I'll know I'm a good person because I am spiritual." Jesus says, "I don't want you to simply shift from one performance-based identity to another; I want you to find a whole new way. I want you to lose the old self, the old identity, and base yourself and your identity on me and the gospel." I love the fact that he says "for me and for the gospel." He is reminding us not to be abstract about this. You can't just say, "Oh, I see: I can't build my identity on my parents' approval because that comes and goes; I can't build my life on my career success; I can't build my life on romance. Instead I will build my life on God." If that's as far as you take it, God is almost an abstraction; and so building your life on him is just an act of the will. And no one has ever been deeply changed by an act of the will. The only thing that can reforge and change a life at its root is love.

Jesus is saying, "It's not enough just to know me as a teacher or as an abstract principle; you have to look at my life. I went to the cross—and on the cross I lost my identity so you can have one."

Once you see the Son of God loving you like that, once you are moved by that viscerally and existentially, you begin to get a strength, an assurance, a sense of your own value and distinctiveness that is not based on what you're doing or whether somebody loves you, whether you've lost weight or how much money you've got. You're free—the old approach to identity is gone. Nobody put this better than C. S. Lewis in the last two pages of his

Mere Christianity, where he comments on Jesus's call to lose yourself to find yourself:

> The more we get what we now call "ourselves" out of the way and let Him take us over, the more truly ourselves we become . . . our real selves are all waiting for us in him. . . . The more I resist Him and try to live on my own, the more I become dominated by my own heredity and upbringing and surrounding and natural desires. In fact what I so proudly call "Myself" becomes merely the meeting-place for trains of events which I never started and I cannot stop. What I call "My wishes" become merely the desires thrown up by my physical organism or pumped into me by other men's thoughts. . . . It is when I turn to Christ, when I give myself up to His personality, that I finally begin to have a real personality all of my own. . . . [Nevertheless], you must not go to Christ for the sake of [a new self]. As long as your own personality is what you are bothering about you are not going to Him at all.[45]

If you go to Jesus to get a new personality, Lewis says, you still haven't really gone to Jesus. Your real self will not come out as long as you are looking for it; it will only emerge when you're looking for him.

When Peter hears that Jesus is going to Jerusalem, which will entail suffering—almost certainly not just for Jesus but also for him—he's furious. Why? Because he had an agenda, and his agenda led from strength to strength and it didn't include suffering. When he sees that Jesus is not working from his agenda, he rebukes him. If your agenda is the end, then Jesus is just the means; you're using him. But if Jesus is the King, you cannot

make him a means to your end. You can't come to a king negotiating. You lay your sword at a king's feet and say, "Command
me." If you try to negotiate instead, if you say, "I'll obey you
if . . . ," you aren't recognizing him as a king. But don't forget
this: Jesus is not just a king; he's a king on a cross. If he were only
a king on a throne, you'd submit to him just because you have
to. But he's a king who went to the cross for you. Therefore you
can submit to him out of love and trust. This means coming to
him not negotiating but saying, "Lord, whatever you ask I will
do, whatever you send I will accept." When someone gave himself utterly for you, how can you not give yourself utterly to him?
Taking up your cross means for you to die to self-determination,
die to control of your own life, die to using him for your agenda.

When Jesus says, "I tell you the truth, some who are standing
here who will not taste death before they see the kingdom of God
come with power," what does he mean? Some people have inter-
preted this to mean that the current generation wouldn't pass
away before he returned to earth. But that's not what he's saying.
The early church cherished this passage well beyond the death of
Jesus's generation. They knew that Jesus meant something else.
They understood him to mean that although the kingdom of
God began in weakness—on the cross—it would not end that
way. They would see the power of his resurrection, and see the
church multiply and grow in love, and service, and influence in
the world.[46]

For us, the kingdom of God begins with weakness, relin-
quishment, giving up our rights to our own life; it begins with
admitting that we need a Savior. We need someone to actually
fulfill all the requirements and pay for our sin. That's weakness.
Jesus started in weakness—first, by becoming human, and second, by going to a cross. And if we want him in our life, we have
to start in weakness too. The kingdom begins there, but it won't

end there. Someday, when Jesus returns and ushers in a renewed creation, love will totally triumph over hate and life will totally triumph over death.

Lewis closes his passage about "losing your life to find it" with this:

> Give up yourself, and you will find your real self. Lose your life and you will save it. Submit to death, the death of your ambitions and favorite wishes every day and the death of your whole body in the end: Submit with every fiber of your being, and you will find eternal life. Keep back nothing. Nothing that you have not given away will be really yours. Nothing in you that has not died will ever be raised from the dead. Look for yourself, and you will find in the long run only hatred, loneliness, despair, rage, ruin, and decay. But look for Christ and you will find Him, and with Him everything else thrown in.[47]

You see, if there really is a dance, then there really is a King who loves us without need. And if there really is a stain we can't wash out, then there is going to have to be a cross.

PART TWO

THE CROSS

The Purpose of Jesus

TEN

THE MOUNTAIN

As soon as Peter confesses that Jesus is the Christ, the focus changes. I said at the outset that while the first half of the book of Mark centers on who Jesus is, the second half of the book centers on his purpose—what he came to do. In the first half we see that he is both God and man, the eternal King. He is forgiveness, rest, power, and unbounded love. Yet at this point in the life of Jesus, readers of Mark are left with a lot of questions about what he has come to do and how he will do it.

But as soon as Peter says, "You are the Christ," Jesus immediately explains that he has to die. Jesus will now speak constantly of his death and suffering, in ways that the disciples find extremely hard to swallow. So the second half of Mark's Gospel will show us why the cross was necessary and what it accomplished. What seemed like it might become a story of triumph is going to look more and more like a tragedy.

Now that Jesus has begun revealing more details about his mission, he also becomes more explicit about what it means to follow him. In the first half of Mark, he called people to follow him, but now he is painting a more vivid picture of what that following entails. As he takes up a cross, we must do the same. As the cross and glory are linked in his life, so the cross and glory will be linked in our lives. That is the theme that is introduced to us in the second half of Mark, beginning here:

> *After six days Jesus took Peter, James, and John with him and led them up a high mountain, where they were all alone. There he was transfigured before them. His clothes became dazzling white, whiter than anyone in the world could bleach them. And there appeared before them Elijah and Moses, who were talking with Jesus. Peter said to Jesus, "Rabbi, it is good for us to be here. Let us put up three shelters—one for you, one for Moses, and one for Elijah." (He did not know what to say, they were so frightened.) Then a cloud appeared and enveloped them, and a voice came from the cloud: "This is my Son, whom I love. Listen to him!" Suddenly, when they looked around, they no longer saw anyone with them except Jesus.*
>
> (Mark 9:2–8)

Centuries prior to this event, according to the book of Exodus in the Old Testament, God came down on Mount Sinai in a cloud. The voice of God spoke out of the cloud, and everyone was afraid. Moses went to the top of the mountain and begged to see God's glory: "Show me your glory—your infinite greatness and unimaginable beauty." And God responded, "When my glory passes by, I will put you in a cleft in the rock and cover you with my hand until I have passed by, but my face cannot be seen. No one may see me and live" (Exodus 33:18–23). Moses was not able to see God's glory directly. But even getting near was enough to make Moses's face shine with the reflected glory of God.

Now, centuries later, we're on top of another mountain and there's glory again. This dazzling brightness makes Jesus's clothes "whiter than anyone in the world could bleach them." There's a mountain, a voice out of a cloud—and even Moses makes an appearance. Is this Mount Sinai all over again? No, because there's a head-snapping twist. Moses had reflected the glory of God as the moon reflects the light of the sun. But Jesus *produces* the unsurpassable glory of God; it emanates from him. Jesus does not *point to* the glory of God as Elijah, Moses, and every other prophet has done; Jesus *is* the glory of God in human form. The author of the book of Hebrews puts it like this: "The Son [Jesus] is the radiance of God's glory and the exact representation of his being" (Hebrews 1:3).

Something else happens here that never happened on Mount Sinai—Peter, James, and John are in the presence of God and yet they do not die.

On Mount Sinai, God came down as a cloud. It was called "the *shekinah* glory"; do you remember it from the holy of holies where the high priest atoned for the sins of the people of Israel? He spoke out of the cloud—it was his raw presence, which the Israelites knew was fatal. When God told Moses, "No one can see my face and live," he was saying that there's an infinite gap between deity and humanity. "You can't take my reality," said God; "you can't endure the presence of my holiness, my glory. It would destroy you."

This is why, here on the mountain where Jesus is "transfig-ured" (this scene is generally known as the transfiguration), Peter is scared. So scared he doesn't know what he's saying, accord-ing to Mark. He stammers out, "Rabbi . . . let us put up three shelters—one for you, one for Moses, and one for Elijah." To us that's a baffling proposal—so let's explore it.

The word translated *shelters* here is actually the Greek word for *tabernacle*. After God's glory came down on Mount Sinai, the Hebrew people built a tabernacle. Why? Most religions have recognized that there's a wide gap of some kind between deity and humanity. Therefore many religions have temples (or tabernacles) with priests and sacrifices and rituals to transform your consciousness or take away your sin—to mediate the gap and protect human beings from the divine presence. What Peter is actually saying here is, "We need a tabernacle, we need to set up rituals, to protect us from the presence of God." Immediately after Peter says this, a cloud appears and envelops Jesus, Moses, and Elijah. And from within the *shekinah* glory cloud, God says, "This is my Son, whom I love. Listen to him!" They are in the very presence of God. Yet Peter, James, and John do not die. How could that be? "Suddenly, when they looked around, they no longer saw anyone with them except Jesus." That's Mark's way of saying: Moses is gone, Elijah is gone, and Jesus is the bridge over the gap between God and humanity. Jesus is able to give what Elijah couldn't give, what Moses couldn't give, what no one else could ever deliver. Through Jesus, we can cross the gap into the very heart of reality, into the steps of the dance. Jesus is the temple and tabernacle to end all temples and tabernacles, because he is the sacrifice to end all sacrifices, the ultimate priest to point the way for all priests.

When the cloud comes down, not only do the disciples not die, they are surrounded and embraced by the brilliance of God. They hear God the Father speaking of his love for the Son, just as he did when Jesus was baptized at the beginning of Mark. Then suddenly the cloud goes away, and they are left standing there blinking in the comparatively dim light of the mountaintop, in a state of electrified wonder.

James, Peter, and John have experienced *worship.*

Worship is a preview of the thing that all of our hearts are longing for, whether we know it or not. We seek it in art, in romance, in the arms of our lovers, in our family. In his famous sermon "The Weight of Glory," C. S. Lewis says:

> The sense that in this universe we are treated as strang-
> ers, the longing to be acknowledged, to meet with some
> response, to bridge some chasm that yawns between us
> and reality, is part of our inconsolable secret. And surely
> from this point of view the promise of glory becomes
> highly relevant to our deepest desire. For glory means
> good [rapport] with God, acceptance by God, response,
> acknowledgment, and welcome into the heart of things.
> The door on which we have been knocking all our lives
> will open at last. . . . then our lifelong nostalgia, our long-
> ing to be reunited with something in the universe from
> which we now feel cut off, to be on the inside of some
> door which we have always seen from the outside, is no
> mere neurotic fancy but the truest index of our real situ-
> ation. . . . At present we are on the outside of the world,
> the wrong side of the door. . . . but all the leaves of the
> New Testament are rustling with the rumor that it will
> not always be so. Some day, God willing, we shall get *in.*[48]

Worship is not just believing. Before they went up the mountain, Peter, James, and John already believed in God. And Peter
had already said, "You are the Christ." But now they have sensed
it. The presence of God has enveloped them. They have had a

foretaste of what Lewis says all of us are longing for: the very face and embrace of God.

The Death of Glory

Imagine the scene afterward, when the echo of God's voice has finally faded. The disciples must have had a dozen questions for Jesus. Mark recounts what happens next:

> *As they were coming down the mountain, Jesus gave them orders not to tell anyone what they had seen until the Son of Man had risen from the dead. They kept the matter to themselves, discussing what "rising from the dead" meant. And they asked him, "Why do the teachers of the law say that Elijah must come first?" Jesus replied, "To be sure, Elijah does come first, and restores all things. Why then is it written that the Son of Man must suffer much and be rejected? But I tell you, Elijah has come, and they have done to him everything they wished, just as it is written about him."*
>
> (Mark 9:9–13)

As they come down off the mountain, Jesus instructs the disciples: "Don't tell anybody about this till the resurrection." Why? The full meaning of this episode would only be apparent after the resurrection because the transfiguration is a glimpse, a preview, of the resurrection (and of the second coming, Jesus's return to restore the world at the end of time, prophesied in the Book of Revelation at the end of the Bible). Also, until the resurrection, who in the world would believe it?

One thing is clear to the disciples, though. By speaking of his resurrection here, Jesus is again pointing to his death. Remember that when Jesus told them, "I'm the Messiah, but I'm going to suffer and die," Peter rebuked Jesus. Here again Peter and the others push back, but this time they're a little more cagey: "Why do the teachers of the law say that Elijah must come first?" they ask.

The Old Testament book of Malachi prophesied that Elijah would return before the great Day of the Lord, when God will appear and make everything right. So the disciples are saying, "Hey, we just saw Elijah up there. The Day of the Lord must be near! Why all this talk about death? Elijah is here." Jesus lays them flat: "I tell you, Elijah has come, and they have done to him everything they wished, just as it is written about him." Jesus is saying, "The Elijah that the prophet was pointing to was John the Baptist, and he has suffered and died. Elijah has come and gone." And he repeats that "it is written that the Son of Man must suffer much." Just as Elijah's coming was a herald of the Lord's coming, so Elijah's execution (John the Baptist had been beheaded by Herod) is a herald of the Lord's execution.

When Jesus was baptized in the opening chapter of Mark, the Spirit descended on him like a dove, and it fortified him to begin teaching and healing publicly. Now the Father envelops him with his presence—the light and the *shekinah* glory and the voice—to fortify him for the far greater test that awaits him as he moves resolutely toward his execution on the cross. And it's not only Jesus who is strengthened by the experience: God is also preparing the disciples for the test they will face when their leader is taken from them.

Have you ever had that kind of experience? When the compassion and love of another person helped you deal with your suffering? When someone's unconditional approval and encouragement transformed your fear into resolve? When an encounter with beauty seemed to neutralize your anxiety and give you hope?

And if you got that kind of help more often, wouldn't you be different? Wouldn't trouble make you wiser, deeper, and stronger instead of bitter and hard and joyless? Wouldn't suffering make you more compassionate, rather than more cynical about human nature? Wouldn't failure be more likely to be productive in your life? Of course it would.

But here's the question: How are you going to get more of that kind of approval, that kind of encouragement, that kind of love, without burning out your friends and family with your neediness?

The answer for us, as it was for the disciples, is *worship*. You must have access through worship to the very presence of God. You have to see clearly in your mind what God has done and is doing through Jesus. You have to experience foretastes of that embrace God is going to give you someday. You need to actually *sense* what you know of God's love.

It's one thing to be told that somebody is remarkably attractive. You believe it, but when you actually see him or her up close, you say, "Oh, *wow*." What happened? Did you get new information? No—you're *experiencing* what you already knew to be true. Somebody says, "This restaurant is unbelievable; it's the best." You believe what you're told, but when you go there and eat, you're still bowled over. Did you get new information? No—you're *experiencing* what you already knew to be true. It's one thing to know that the glorious Creator God loves you, cares for you, holds you, but it's another thing to sense it, to experience it. Whatever life brings you, you will need those foretastes to nourish and strengthen you.

The transfiguration is not just a miraculous parlor trick to convince the disciples of Jesus's deity. It is an experience of collective worship that they are going to need for what's ahead.

A Glimpse of Glory

How, then, can we have access to the presence of God in that way? How can we have these foretastes? Jesus and the disciples are barely off the mountain before he gets the chance to show us how to make our way into God's presence.

> *When they came to the other disciples, they saw a large crowd around them and the teachers of the law arguing with them. As soon as all the people saw Jesus, they were overwhelmed with wonder and ran to greet him. "What are you arguing with them about?" he asked. A man in the crowd answered, "Teacher, I brought you my son, who is possessed by a spirit that has robbed him of speech. Whenever it seizes him, it throws him to the ground. He foams at the mouth, gnashes his teeth and becomes rigid. I asked your disciples to drive out the spirit, but they could not."*
>
> (Mark 9:14–18)

A big argument is going on among the teachers of the law and a crowd of other people and Jesus's disciples—those who hadn't gone up the mountain. They're trying to exorcise a demon, and it's not working. Evil is present, and everybody's confused.

Again, Mark takes the existence of demonic activity—of a continued battle against evil, personal supernatural beings—as a self-evident aspect of reality, a fact of life. Not everyone is personally possessed by a demon like the boy in this story, but Paul says in Ephesians 6 and elsewhere that we are all fighting demonic "principalities" all the time. Remember that even Jesus was not immune to their attacks. We read early on in the book of Mark that just after his baptism Jesus "was in the desert forty days, being tempted by Satan" (Mark 1:12).

The boy in this story is possessed by a demon, making him deaf and mute and causing convulsions. It is an overwhelming physical and spiritual condition that not only renders the boy helpless, but also stymies everyone around him—his father, the disciples, and the teachers of the law. The story continues:

"O unbelieving generation," Jesus replied, "how long shall I stay with you? How long shall I put up with you? Bring the boy to me." So they brought him. When the spirit saw Jesus, it immediately threw the boy into a convulsion. He fell to the ground and rolled around, foaming at the mouth. Jesus asked the boy's father, "How long has he been like this?" "From childhood," he answered. "It has often thrown him into fire or water to kill him. But if you can do anything, take pity on us and help us." "'If you can'?" said Jesus. "Everything is possible for him who believes." Immediately the boy's father exclaimed, "I do believe; help me overcome my unbelief!" When Jesus saw that a crowd was running to the scene, he rebuked the evil spirit. "You deaf and mute spirit," he said, "I command you, come out of him and never enter him again." The spirit shrieked, convulsed him violently, and came out. The boy looked so much like a corpse that many said, "He's dead." But Jesus took him by the hand and lifted him to his feet, and he stood up. After Jesus had gone indoors, his disciples asked him privately, "Why couldn't we drive it out?" He replied, "This kind can come out only by prayer."

(Mark 9:19–29)

The disciples are trying to exorcise a demon. But they have been trying to exorcise it *without praying*. How arrogant, how clueless they are about their inadequacy to deal with the evil and suffering of the world. The disciples tried prayerless exorcism for the same reason that they couldn't understand why Jesus had to die—they didn't see how weak and proud they were. They underestimated the power of evil in the world and in themselves.

The teachers of the law are there too, probably criticizing. Only one figure in this entire scene is acknowledging his weakness, admitting that he does not have what it takes to handle the suffering and evil that he faces—the father of the boy.

This man asks Jesus, "Would you heal my son?" And Jesus says, "Everything is possible for him who believes." That is, "I can do it if you can believe." The father responds, "I do believe; help me overcome my unbelief!"—that is, "I'm trying but I'm full of doubts." Then Jesus heals the man's son. This is very good news. Through Jesus we don't need perfect righteousness, just repentant helplessness, to access the presence of God.

Jesus could have told the man, "I am the glory of God in human form. Purify your heart, confess all your sins, get rid of all your doubts and your double-mindedness. Once you have surrendered to me totally and can come before me with a pure heart, then you can ask for the healing you need." But Jesus doesn't say that—not at all. The boy's father says, "I'm *not* faithful, I am riddled with doubts, and I cannot muster the strength necessary to meet my moral and spiritual challenges. But help me." That's saving faith—faith in Jesus instead of in oneself. Perfect righteousness is impossible for us, and if you wait for that, you will never come into the presence of God. You must admit that you are *not* righteous, and that you need help. When you can say *that*, you are approaching God to worship.

But we cannot leave this scene without an acute awareness of what Jesus is about to lose. He has lived for endless ages in glory with the Father. On the mountain we see Jesus surrounded by

God; on the cross he will be forsaken. On the mountain we see the life he has always led—embraced and clothed with the love and light of God—but on the cross he will be naked in the dark.

Why did Jesus put himself through that? He did it for us. Paul tells us clearly that evil is unmasked and defeated on our behalf at the cross. He writes in his letter to the church at Colossae that Jesus "disarmed the power and authorities . . . triumphing over them by the cross" (Colossians 2:15).

And on the mountain, through the Spirit, God was strengthening Jesus for his mission, for the infinite suffering he would endure to defeat all evil. And God can empower us in the same way to face evil and overcome our own suffering.

You may know in your head that God loves you—but sometimes the Spirit makes it especially clear to you that that is the case. Sometimes you go to the mountain. Sometimes through the Spirit you can hear God make a statement of unconditional, permanent, intimate love. Sometimes you don't just *know about* God's love but in your heart you actually hear God saying, "You're my daughter, you're my son, I love you. I would go to infinite cost and infinite depths not to lose you—and I have."

When you have pursued God in repentant helplessness, you will have worshipped. And every time you sense his embrace, your soul will shine the slightest bit brighter with his reflected glory, and you will be the slightest bit more ready to face what life has in store for you.

ELEVEN

✦✦✦✦✦

THE TRAP

In an interview Andrew Walls, a distinguished historian of world Christianity, noted that wherever the other great world religions began, that is still their center today. Islam started in Arabia, at Mecca, and the Middle East is still the center of Islam today. Buddhism started in the Far East, and that's still the center of Buddhism. So too with Hinduism—it began in India and it is still predominantly an Indian religion. Christianity is the exception; Christianity's center is always moving, always on a pilgrimage. The original center of Christianity was Jerusalem, but then the Hellenistic Gentiles, who were considered the unwashed barbarians, embraced Christianity with such force that soon the center of Christianity moved to the Hellenistic Mediterranean world—to Alexandria, North Africa, and Rome—and it stayed there for a number of centuries. But then another set of unwashed barbarians, the northern Europeans—Franks and Anglo-Saxons and Celts—so took hold of Christian faith that soon the center of Christianity migrated again, to northern Europe. There (and in North America, through colonization and immigration) the center has rested for a thousand years, but recently it is shifting again.

In the twentieth century, Christianity receded in Europe, and in North America it just barely kept up with the population growth. Meanwhile, in Latin America, Asia, and Africa, it has been growing at up to ten times the population growth rate. In the past decade a major corner was turned: More than 50 percent of Christians in the world now live in the southern hemisphere.

For example, at the turn of this century, in the United States there were roughly 2.5 million Episcopalians and other Anglicans. In Nigeria alone there were 17 million Anglicans; in Uganda there were 8 million. Thus in just those two countries there live more than ten times the number in the United States. In the year 1900, Africa was only 1 percent Christian. Now Christians make up nearly half the African population.[49]

In the next fifty to seventy years, the center of Christianity is predicted to complete this shift away from European countries and from the United States. It will migrate, as it always migrates.

In the interview with Andrew Walls, he was asked, "Why does this happen? If the centers of other religions remain constant, why does the center of Christianity constantly change?" Walls replied, "One must conclude, I think, that there is a certain vulnerability, a fragility, at the heart of Christianity. You might say that this is the vulnerability of the cross."[50] The heart of the gospel is the cross, and the cross is all about giving up power, pouring out resources, and serving. Walls hinted that when Christianity is in a place of power and wealth for a long period, the radical message of sin and grace and the cross can become muted or even lost. Then Christianity starts to transmute into a nice, safe religion, one that's for respectable people who try to be good. And eventually it becomes virtually dormant in those places and the center moves somewhere else.

Caught in the Trap

Walls asserts that the center of Christianity is always migrating away from power and wealth. This story in Mark helps us understand why:

> *As Jesus started on his way, a man ran up to him and fell on his knees before him. "Good teacher," he asked, "what must I do to inherit eternal life?"*
>
> (Mark 10:17)

In parallel accounts in other Gospels we learn that this was a young man, and also that he was a ruler; so he is often called the Rich Young Ruler. Mark continues:

> *"Why do you call me good?" Jesus answered. "No one is good—except God alone. You know the commandments: 'Do not murder, do not commit adultery, do not steal, do not give false testimony, do not defraud, honor your father and mother.'" "Teacher," he declared, "all these I have kept since I was a boy." Jesus looked at him and loved him. "One thing you lack," he said. "Go, sell everything you have and give to the poor, and you will have treasure in heaven. Then come, follow me." At this the man's face fell. He went away sad, because he had great wealth.*
>
> (Mark 10:18–22)

Jesus tells this spiritual seeker something that he can't accept, and as the man walks away, notice the disciples' reaction:

> *Jesus looked around and said to his disciples, "How hard it is for the rich to enter the kingdom of God!" The disciples were amazed at his words. But Jesus said again, "Children, how hard it is to enter the kingdom of God! It is easier for a camel to go through the eye of a needle than for a rich man to enter the kingdom of God."*
>
> (Mark 10:23–25)

Have you noticed that some of Jesus's sayings are like hard candy? They're not like chocolate, which you can let melt in your mouth, swallow, and it's gone—a momentary pleasure. With a hard candy, if you try to take it in too fast, you're likely headed for the dentist's chair or the Heimlich Maneuver. Many of Jesus's sayings are like that. You work on them, you work into them, and you work through them, and only then are you rewarded with layer after layer of increasing sweetness. Jesus delivers a famously hard saying here: "It is easier for a camel to go through the eye of a needle than for a rich man to enter the kingdom of God." The statement is as controversial now as it was at the time he made it. Again note the disciples' reaction:

> *Jesus said again, "Children, how hard it is to enter the kingdom of God! It is easier for a camel to go through the eye of a needle than for a rich man to enter the kingdom of God." The disciples were even more amazed, and said to each other, "Who then can be saved?" Jesus looked at them and said, "With man this is impossible, but not with God; all things are possible with God."*
>
> (Mark 10:24–27)

There are many who believe that you can't accrue great wealth without taking advantage of people. This is the premise behind many political and economic philosophies: that nobody can get rich without stepping on others. Even *having* a lot of wealth is seen as an injustice. You might expect the disciples to say, "Excellent, Jesus! We're glad you're not going to let any of the rich into your kingdom—they've gotten away with their exploitation long enough." But that's not their response. Instead they say, "If *he* can't be saved, who can?" The disciples came from a culture that did not see wealth as evil, but rather as the reward for moral behavior. They accepted the view that if you live a good life, then God will reward you with prosperity. This was the worldview, for example, of Job's friends in the Old Testament book of Job. They assumed that material prosperity meant you were living a good life and God was pleased, while poverty was a sign that you were not living a good life and God was not pleased. But Jesus's response to this man shows he does not subscribe to these simplistic views—neither is great wealth necessarily exploitative, nor is it always a sign of virtue and God's favor.

Look at how Jesus deals with the man in this passage. By referring to several of the Ten Commandments, Jesus asks him some implicit questions. For example, "Do not defraud." In other words, have you misrepresented the facts in business dealings? "Do not steal, do not give false testimony": Jesus is asking, "Have you stolen? Have you even exploited? Have you taken from people things that are by rights theirs?"

The young man says, "All these [commandments] I have kept since I was a boy." That is: "No, with all my wealth I have always acted in justice and kindness and fairness; I have never sinned in any of these ways."

Jesus doesn't turn to him and say, "Liar." He accepts the assertion. While of course you can accumulate wealth through vice, it is possible to earn wealth through virtue and hold it in virtue—that is, discipline, vision, delayed gratification, patience. Here we see that Jesus has no ideological problem with wealth creation per se. He does not say that having money is wrong or unjust in itself.

Nonetheless, he says it is harder for a camel to go through the eye of a needle than for a rich person to get into the kingdom of God.

And over the centuries people have tried to deal with this statement, sometimes in funny ways. Some people say, "Well, it's not a literal needle. Back in Jesus's day Jerusalem's walls had gates that were very narrow, and it was hard to get a camel through, especially if it was carrying a large load. But if you took the load off and the camel held its breath as you pushed, it was hard but not impossible for it to get through the gate." Or, "It's not a literal camel; there's an Aramaic word for *twine* that sounds a lot like the Aramaic word for *camel*. What Jesus is really trying to say is that it's very difficult to get twine through the eye of a needle, but if you suck on it and point it with great care, it's not impossible."

Those explanations overreach; I think it's clear what Jesus means by this image. Every culture has vivid metaphors like this. Think of the saying "a snowball's chance." It is impossible for a snowball to survive in a hot place, and it is impossible to get a camel through the eye of a needle. Just so, it is *impossible* for the rich to get into the kingdom of God. That's what Jesus is saying.

But there is an important nuance here. Jesus didn't mean that it's a sin to be rich. It is not that all individual rich people are bad, nor are all individual poor people good. Jesus did not make such blanket assertions. Nor, on the other hand, was he saying, "Just be careful, don't fall into greed, be generous from time to time." No. Jesus was saying that there is something radically wrong with *all* of us—but money has particular power to blind us to it. In fact, it has so much power to deceive us of our true spiritual state that we need a gracious, miraculous intervention from God to see it. It's impossible without God, without a miracle. Without grace.

Revealing the Trap

Consider how Jesus counseled this young man. Yes, this man needed counseling, though on the outside he looked completely pulled together. He was rich, he was young, and he was probably good-looking—it's hard to be rich and young and *not* be good-looking. But he didn't have it all together. If he had, he would never have come to Jesus and asked, "What must I do to inherit eternal life?"

Any devout Jew would have known the answer to this question. The rabbis were always posing this question in their writings and their teachings. And their answer was always the same; there were no differing schools of thought on this one. The answer was "Obey the statutes of God and avoid all sin." The young man would have known this answer. Why then was he asking Jesus?

Jesus's perceptive statement "One thing you lack" allows us to capture the gist of the young man's struggle. The man was saying, "You know what, I've done everything right: I've been successful economically, successful socially, successful morally, successful religiously. I've heard you're a good rabbi, and I'm wondering if there's something I've missed, something I'm over-looking. I sense that something is lacking."

Of course he was missing something. Because anyone who counts on what they are *doing* to get eternal life will find that, in spite of everything they've accomplished, there's an emptiness, an insecurity, a doubt. Something is bound to be missing. How can anyone ever know whether they are good enough?

In New York City, as you walk down the street, you see a lot of people with flawless faces. You can't do it unless you want to be arrested for harassment, but you'd like to go up to some of them and say, "Are you quite as flawless as you look?" They would have to say no, because every day they look at themselves in the mirror and they know their little scars and deformities. In fact, one of the reasons many of them are so beautiful is that they've put tremendous time, energy, and resources into covering their blemishes. Still, if you look closely enough at anything or anyone, you will see flaws and pockmarks.

Here's a man who is pulled together, has degrees from the right places, is on the partnership track, has already made millions, and is only twenty-eight years old. Yet, to his surprise, he finds himself seeking out gurus and rabbis and saying, "I'm still missing something. Do you know of anything I'm missing? I've accomplished a lot but I sense there's one more thing I need to do. I'm ready to open up a spiritual portfolio. What do I have to put in there? I'm willing to make some changes. Just tell me what to do."

Jesus tells him. And his counsel lays the man flat.

Jesus begins his reply by telegraphing the punch. The first thing he says to the man is "Why do you call me good? No one is good—except God alone." That's a hint, a preview. Jesus is not saying that he's not good. He doesn't say, "Why are you calling me good? I, Jesus, am not." He is saying, "Why are you walking up to somebody you think is just a normal human rabbi and calling him good? There's a flaw in your whole idea of goodness and badness." That's the hint.

But then the blow comes. Jesus has already accepted what the man said about having obeyed the commandments, having lived an ethical life. What Jesus says to the man goes further. Jesus proceeds to tell the young man the one thing he needs to do:

"Go, sell everything you have and give to the poor, and you will have treasure in heaven. Then come, follow me."

In other words Jesus says: "If you want to follow me and to have eternal life, of course you shouldn't commit adultery; you shouldn't defraud people or murder them. You shouldn't do bad things. But if you just repent of doing bad things, all it will do is make you a religious person. If you want eternal life, if you want intimacy with God, if you want to get over that nagging sense that there's still something missing, if you can't find a way to get the stain out, then you have to change how you relate to your gifts and your successes. You have to repent of how you've been using your *good things*."

And there are many ways that we use these "good things." We may be using our "good things" to deal with the imperfections that no one else can see. We may be incessantly trying to turn material wealth into a spiritual treasure to deal with that inner sense of poverty. We may be trying to turn physical beauty into spiritual beauty to deal with that inner sense of deformity. We also may be using our good things to feel superior to others, or to get them to do the things we want them to do. Most of all, we may point to our good things—our achievements and our attainments—and say to God, "Look at what I've accomplished! You owe it to me to answer my prayers." We may use our good things to get control of God and other people.

So Jesus is saying to the man in this passage, "You have put your faith and trust in your wealth and accomplishments. But the effort is alienating you from God. Right now God is your boss; but God is not your Savior, and here's how you can see it: *I want you to imagine life without money.* I want you to imagine all of it gone. No inheritance, no inventory, no servants, no mansions— all of that is gone. All you have is me. Can you live like that?"

How does the man respond to Jesus's counseling? "He went away sad." The word *sad* translated here is better translated "grieved"—he *grieved*. Let me tell you why that translation is better. There's a place where the same Greek word is applied to Jesus. Matthew records in his Gospel that in the Garden of Gethsemane Jesus started to sweat blood as he *grieved in deep distress.* Why? He knew he was about to experience the ultimate dislocation, the ultimate disorientation. He was about to lose the joy of his life, the core of his identity. He was going to lose his Father. Jesus was losing his spiritual center, his very self.

When Jesus called this young man to give up his money, the man started to grieve, because money was for him what the Father was for Jesus. It was the center of his identity. To lose his money would have been to lose himself—to lose what little sense he had of having covered the stain.

It's one thing to have God as a boss, an example, a mentor; but if you want God to be your Savior, you have to replace what you're already looking to as a savior. Everybody's got something. What is it for you?

If you want to be a Christian, of course you'll repent of your sins. But after you've repented of your sins you'll have to repent of how you have used the good things in your life to fill the place where God should be. If you want intimacy with God, if you want to get over this sense that something is missing, it will have to become God that you love with all your heart and strength.

Do you see how nuanced Jesus's reply is? This young man's problem is not his financial worth; it's his moral worth. It's his sense that he doesn't need the grace of God. Christians, you see, are *people who know that their Christianity is impossible, a miracle*—there's nothing natural about it, it flies in the face of all one's merits. Everybody has to recognize that we have been resting our hopes on some form of personal merit. And it's our personal merit, our moral worth, that keeps us from understanding the cross.

What happens with the young ruler is analogous to another, less confrontational encounter recounted a bit later, in Mark chapter 12. In that case, as in the first one, Jesus shows that the law demands that we give God everything. A teacher of the law is impressed with Jesus's wisdom. So he, like the rich young man, asks Jesus a question:

> One of the teachers of the law came and heard them debating. Noticing that Jesus had given them a good answer, he asked him, "Of all the commandments, which is the most important?"
>
> (Mark 12:28)

This inquiry is designed to trip Jesus up, but it seems also to be sincere—he really does want to know the answer. The teachers of the law were professional scribes and scholars of the law. They spent their lives studying, classifying, and categorizing it. Some had discerned as many as 613 rules in the Old Testament law. And they were always trying to distinguish the lighter ones from the heavier ones. The fundamental question was: "Of all the hundreds of rules and commands, which one is the most important?" This is how Jesus responds:

> "The most important one," answered Jesus, "is this: 'Hear, O Israel, the Lord our God, the Lord is one. Love the Lord your God with all your heart and with all your soul and with all your mind and with all your strength.'

The second is this: 'Love your neighbor as yourself.' There is no commandment greater than these."

(Mark 12:29–31)

Jesus answers with two commands from the Hebrew Scriptures. The first is from Deuteronomy 6:4–5. This passage includes the *shema*, which pious Jews recited morning and evening, as well as the command to love God with all our being. The second he takes from Leviticus 19:18, to love our neighbor as much as we love ourselves. Thus Jesus boils down all of the law of God into one principle—love, directed to God and to others. Here Jesus is going to the very heart of the core dilemma of ethics. Human thinkers have for centuries felt there was a tension between "Law" and "Love." Do I do the legal thing, or the loving thing? Jesus is not so much picking one or two rules over the others, nor is he choosing love over law, but rather he is showing that love is what fulfills the law. The law is not being fulfilled unless it is obeyed as a way of giving and showing love to God or others.

When he hears Jesus's reply, does this man walk away sad like the rich young ruler? Mark continues:

"Well said, teacher," the man replied. "You are right in saying that God is one and there is no other but him. To love him with all your heart, with all your understanding and with all your strength, and to love your neighbor as yourself is more important than all burnt offerings and sacrifices."

(Mark 12:32–33)

The teacher admits that these two commands are the most important. His reference to the burnt offerings and sacrifices shows that he realizes that these cannot make up for sins. Here we see him coming to recognize what an impossible standard the law gives us—that it is easier for a camel to go through the eye of a needle than for a good man to satisfy the law. The closer he gets to seeing this, the closer he is to figuring out the gospel. If we concentrate on rules and regulations exclusively, we can begin to feel pretty righteous, but when we look at the heart attitude that the law really is requiring and getting at, we begin to realize how much we need grace and mercy.

And what was Jesus's assessment?

> *When Jesus saw that he had answered wisely, he said to him, "You are not far from the kingdom of God."*
>
> (Mark 12:34)

We sense that Jesus's answer—"You're getting close"—might have given this teacher of the law goose bumps. On the surface it was almost the same answer he gave the rich young man—"One thing you lack"—yet that reply was met with something closer to nausea. Similar underlying questions, similar answers, completely different responses. Only one of them could see the trap.

Avoiding the Trap

What is your attitude toward money?

It's not a coincidence that for every one time Jesus warns about building our lives on sex and romance, he warns ten times about money. Money has always been one of the most common saviors. Your ability to go out to cool restaurants, to have nice new things, to negotiate a professional culture and peer group—all those things are probably more important to you than you know.

How do you know that money isn't just money to you? Here are some of the signs: You can't give large amounts of it away. You get scared if you might have less than you're accustomed to having. You see people who are doing better than you, even though you might have worked harder or might be a better person, and it gets under your skin. And when that happens, you have one foot in the trap. Because then it's no longer just a tool; it's the scorecard. It's your essence, your identity. No matter how much money you have, though it's not intrinsically evil, it has incredible power to keep you from God.

But did you notice what Mark wrote as Jesus talked with the rich young ruler: He "looked at him and loved him." Why was Jesus's heart suddenly filled with love? Jesus was a loving man, of course, but this explicit statement of his tenderness toward a specific person is rare in Gospel narratives. Did Jesus love him for his leadership potential? Was it because of what the man said? No, I don't think so.

Jesus, who at this point is about thirty-one years old, looks at him and identifies with him. Jesus, too, is a rich young man, far richer than this man can imagine. Jesus has lived in the incomprehensible glory, wealth, love, and joy of the Trinity from all eternity. He has already left that wealth behind him. Paul says that though Jesus Christ was rich, for our sakes he became poor (2 Corinthians 8:9).

And I'm going into a poverty deeper than anyone has ever known, Jesus says. I am giving it all away. Why? For you. Now, you give away everything to follow me. If I gave away my "big all" to get to you, can you give your "little all" to follow me? I won't ask you to do anything I haven't already done. I'm the ultimate Rich Young Ruler who has given away the ultimate wealth to get you. Now, you need to give away yours to get me."

If you understand that Jesus is the true Rich Young Ruler, it is going to change your attitude to money. For example, you won't be trying to figure out how much you *have* to give away; you'll try to figure out how much you *can* give away. The real standard for how generous you will be is the cross. Jesus is saying, "I want your attitude toward your money to be utterly changed and reworked by what I am going to do there."

Does it move you to think of what Jesus did for you? When that begins to really move you, amaze you, make you weep, you'll have a fighting chance of avoiding the trap. Letting Jesus's sacrifice melt you will drain money of its importance for you. Human status becomes just human status. Approval becomes just approval. You can give money away or you can keep it, depending on what's the best thing at the time. The only way I know to counteract the power of money in your life is to see the ultimate Rich Young Ruler, who gave away everything to come after you, to rescue you, to love you.

Jesus says, "My power is always moving away from people who love power and money. My power is always moving *toward* people who are giving it away, as I did. Where do you want to live?"

TWELVE

THE RANSOM

Jesus does not leave any doubt about what he came to do: He came to die. He tells his disciples repeatedly that this is the case. In fact, by the time of the incident that Mark records below, Jesus has already predicted his death twice: first in Mark chapter 8 after Peter had said, "You are the Christ":

> *[Jesus] then began to teach them that the Son of Man must suffer many things and be rejected by the elders, chief priests, and teachers of the law, and that he must be killed and after three days rise again. He spoke plainly about this. . . .*
>
> (Mark 8:31–32)

Then again in chapter 9:

> *Jesus did not want anyone to know where they were, because he was teaching his disciples. He said to them,*

"The Son of Man is going to be betrayed into the hands of men. They will kill him, and after three days he will rise."

(Mark 9:30–31)

But just in case the disciples (or we) have missed it, Jesus repeats it in chapter 10:

They were on their way up to Jerusalem, with Jesus lead-ing the way, and the disciples were astonished, while those who followed were afraid. Again he took the Twelve aside and told them what was going to happen to him. "We are going up to Jerusalem," he said, "and the Son of Man will be betrayed to the chief priests and teachers of the law. They will condemn him to death and will hand him over to the Gentiles, who will mock him and spit on him, flog him and kill him. Three days later he will rise."

(Mark 10:32–34)

This time, Jesus gives us more details about his death than he had previously. For the first time, we are told that his death will be in Jerusalem, and that both Jews and Gentiles will reject him. Chapter 8 speaks only of the Jewish religious leaders, and 9 speaks more generally about being delivered into the hands of "men." In chapter 8 he had said he would be "rejected" by the priests and scribes, but now he reveals that they will "condemn him to death." This legal term indicates that he will be tried and executed within the criminal justice system. His depiction of his final days also becomes more graphic and violent: They will "mock . . . spit . . . flog" him.

Jesus predicted his death three times in just three chapters— he knew his death was not incidental to his mission. Rather, it was absolutely central to both his identity and his purpose on earth. But the major advance in Mark 10 is that, for the first time, Jesus tells us not only that he will die but why he will do so:

> *"For even the Son of Man did not come to be served, but to serve, and to give his life as a ransom for many."*
>
> (Mark 10:45)

Jesus Christ came not to be served but to die, to give his life. That sets him apart from the founder of every other major religion. Their purpose was to live and be an example; Jesus's purpose was to die and be a sacrifice.

Jesus's choice of the word *come* is a strong giveaway that he existed before he was born: He came into the world. By saying "did not come to be served," he assumes that he had every right to expect to be honored and served when he came, though he did not exercise that privilege.

The final phrase, "to give his life as a ransom for many," sums up the reason why he has to die. Jesus came to be a substitutionary sacrifice. Consider the little preposition *for* in the phrase "a ransom *for* many." In Greek it's the word *anti*, which means "instead of," "in place of," "substitute." What about *ransom*? In English we don't even use that word nowadays except in relation to kidnapping. But here it translates a Greek word, *lutron*, that meant "to buy the freedom of a slave or a prisoner." The ransomer would make a huge sacrificial payment that matched the value, or paid the debt of the slave or the prisoner in order to procure his or her freedom.

Jesus came to pay that kind of ransom. But since the slavery he is dealing with is of a cosmic kind—that is, cosmic evil—it required a cosmic payment. Jesus is saying, "I will pay the ransom

that you couldn't possibly pay, and it will procure your freedom."
The payment is Jesus's death on the cross.

A Willing Sacrifice

This will be hard for you if you're among those who struggle
with the Christian teaching about the cross. It's natural to assume
that the Bible is giving us one more example of those ancient,
primitive, bloodthirsty gods worshiped by those ancient, primitive, bloodthirsty societies. In *The Iliad* by Homer, for example,
Agamemnon didn't get fair winds to Troy until he sacrificed his
daughter. That appeased the wrath of the gods, and then they
let him go to Troy. What Jesus says in Mark may seem to be
just another variation on that theme: a savage ancient culture,
ruled over by an irritable god, demanding blood sacrifices for the
release of innocent slaves and prisoners.

But that's not what's going on here at all. And why not, you
may say? If God is really a loving God, why doesn't he just forgive everybody? Why did Jesus have to go through suffering into
death? Why did he have to be a ransom?

Here's the beginning of an answer: Jesus didn't have to die
despite God's love; he had to die *because* of God's love. And it
had to be this way because *all life-changing love is substitutionary
sacrifice*.

Think about it. If you love a person whose life is all put together
and has no major needs, it costs you nothing. It's delightful.
There are probably four or five people like that where you live.
You ought to find them and become their friend. But if you ever
try to love somebody who has needs, someone who is in trouble
or who is persecuted or emotionally wounded, it's going to cost

you. You can't love them without taking a hit yourself. A transfer of some kind is required, so that somehow their troubles, their problems, transfer to you.

There are a lot of wounded people out there. They are emotionally sinking, they're hurting, and they desperately need to be loved. And when they are with you, you want to look at your watch and make a graceful exit, because listening to them with all their problems can be grueling. It can be exhausting to be a friend to an emotionally damaged person. The only way they're going to start filling up emotionally is if somebody loves them, and the only way to love them is to let yourself be emotionally drained. Some of your fullness is going to have to go into them, and you have to empty out to some degree. If you hold on to your emotional comfort and simply avoid those people, they will sink. The only way to love them is through substitutionary sacrifice.

Or think of an even more dramatic example—parenting. When you have children, they're in a state of dependency. They have so many needs; they can't stand on their own. And they will not just grow out of their dependency automatically. The only way that your children will grow beyond their dependency into self-sufficient adults is for you to essentially abandon your own independence for twenty years or so. When they are young, for example, you've got to read to them and read to them—otherwise they won't develop intellectually. Lots of their books will be boring to you. And you have to listen to your children, and keep listening as they say all kinds of things that make for less than scintillating conversation.

And then there's dressing, bathing, feeding, and teaching them to do these things for themselves. Furthermore, children need about five affirmations for every criticism they hear from you. Unless you sacrifice much of your freedom and a good bit of your time, your children will not grow up healthy and equipped to function. Unfortunately, there are plenty of parents who just won't do it. They won't disrupt their lives that much; they won't pour themselves into their children. They won't make the sacrifice. And their kids grow up physically, but they're still children emotionally—needy, vulnerable, and dependent. Think about it this way: You can make the sacrifice, or they're going to make the sacrifice. It's them or you. Either you suffer temporarily and in a redemptive way, or they're going to suffer tragically, in a wasteful and destructive way. It's at least partly up to you.

All real, life-changing love is substitutionary sacrifice.

Remember Lily Potter, the mother of Harry Potter? In the first book of the series, the evil Lord Voldemort tries to kill Harry, but he can't touch him. When the Voldemort-possessed villain tries to lay hands on Harry, he experiences agonizing pain, and so he is thwarted. Harry later goes to Dumbledore, his mentor, and asks, "Why couldn't he touch me?" Dumbledore replies that "Your mother died to save you. . . . love as powerful as your mother's for you leaves its own mark. Not a scar, no visible sign. . . . [but] to have been loved so deeply . . . will give us some protection forever."[51] Why is Dumbledore's statement so moving? Because we know from experience, from the mundane to the dramatic, that sacrifice is at the heart of real love. And we know that anybody who has ever done anything that made a difference for us—a parent, a teacher, a mentor, a friend, a spouse—sacrificed in some way, stepped in and accepted some hardship so that we would not get hit with it ourselves.

Therefore it makes sense that a God who is more loving than you and I, a God who comes into the world to deal with the ultimate evil, the ultimate sin, would have to make a substitutionary sacrifice. Even we flawed human beings know that you can't just overlook evil. It can't be dealt with, removed, or healed just by saying, "Forget it." It must be paid for, and dealing with it is costly. How much more should we expect that God could not just shrug off evil? The debt had to be paid. But he was so incredibly loving that he was willing to die in order to do it himself.

That's where the God of the Bible is most radically different from the primitive gods of old. The ancients understood the idea of the wrath of God, they understood the idea of justice, the idea of a debt and a necessary punishment, but *they had no idea that God would come and pay it himself.* The cross is the self-substitution of God. That possibility would not have entered into Homer's imagination in a million years, let alone the imagination of Jesus's disciples.

The only way that Jesus could redeem us was to give his life as a ransom. God couldn't just say, "I forgive everybody." In the creation, God could say, "Let there be light," and there was light. God could say, "Let there be vegetation," and there was vegetation. God could say, "Let there be sun, moon, and stars," and there were sun, moon, and stars (Genesis 1). But he couldn't just say, "Let there be forgiveness." That's simply not the way forgiveness works.

God created the world in an instant, and it was a beautiful process. He *re*-created the world on the cross—and it was a horrible process. That's how it works. Love that really changes things and redeems things is always a substitutionary sacrifice.

C. S. Lewis in *The Lion, the Witch and the Wardrobe* puts it like this: "When a willing victim who had committed no treachery was killed in a traitor's stead, the Table would crack and Death itself would start working backward."[52]

A Humble Sacrifice

You would think that by this time the disciples would have grasped the reason Jesus had come and the reason he was going to suffer and die. After all, he'd told them enough times—and Mark records that "He spoke plainly about this." But in the following story it becomes clear that such is not the case. James and John and the other people following Jesus were hearing for at least the third time about his impending and necessary death. Immediately these two disciples have a request for Jesus:

> *Then James and John, the sons of Zebedee, came to him. "Teacher," they said, "we want you to do for us whatever we ask." "What do you want me to do for you?" he asked.*
>
> (Mark 10:35–36)

James and John say, "Teacher, we want you to do for us whatever we ask." That's a great way to start a prayer, don't you think? "Oh Lord, I have a humble request, and I want you to do exactly what I say." Jesus puts up with them graciously—that's the way he was. "What do you want me to do for you?" he asks. He doesn't say, "Um, would you care to start over?" Or "How dare you talk to me like that? Don't you know who I am? Don't you know who you are?" He simply says, "What do you want?"

> *They replied, "Let one of us sit at your right and the other at your left in your glory." "You don't know what you are asking," Jesus said. "Can you drink the cup I drink or be baptized with the baptism I am baptized with?"*
>
> (Mark 10:37–38)

The brothers propose, "Let one of us sit at your right hand and the other at your left in your glory." What are they thinking of? To them, "in your glory" means "when you are seated on your throne," in which case the people on the right and the left are like the prime minister and the chief of staff. John and

James are saying, "When you take power, we would like the top places in your cabinet." Here's the irony of their request. What was Jesus's moment of greatest glory? Where does Jesus most show forth the glory of God's justice? And where does he reveal most profoundly the glory of God's love? On the cross.

When Jesus is at the actual moment of his greatest glory, there *will* be somebody on the right and the left, but they will be criminals being crucified. Jesus says to John and James: *You have no idea what you're asking.*

He speaks to them of the cup and the baptism. In the Hebrew Scriptures *cup* is almost always a metaphor for the just judgment of God against evil. Similarly Jesus uses the word *baptism* in the older sense of an overwhelming experience, an immersion. Jesus is saying, "I am paying that ransom. I am going to drink that cup. I am going to bridge that gap. I will take the just judgment on all human evil. I will take the overwhelming experience of being condemned so that you can be free from all condemnation." But they don't get it. The story continues:

"You don't know what you are asking," Jesus said. "Can you drink the cup I drink or be baptized with the baptism I am baptized with?" "We can," they answered. Jesus said to them, "You will drink the cup I drink and be baptized with the baptism I am baptized with, but to sit at my right or left is not for me to grant. These places belong to those for whom they have been prepared." When the ten heard about this, they became indignant with James and John. Jesus called them together and said, "You know that those who are regarded as rulers of the Gentiles lord it over them, and their high officials exercise authority over them. Not so with you. Instead, whoever wants to become great among you must be your servant, and

whoever wants to be first must be slave of all. For even the Son of Man did not come to be served, but to serve, and to give his life as a ransom for many."

(Mark 10:38–45)

For the disciples, this is yet another lesson on substitutionary sacrifice. But when we read this, we're not supposed to say, "How can these fools keep missing it?" We're supposed to be saying, "What are *we* missing right now?"

Richard Hays, a New Testament scholar, has the following observation about this section of the Gospel of Mark:

> Mark's vision of the moral life is profoundly ironic. Because God's manner of revelation is characterized by hiddenness, reversal, and surprise, those who follow Jesus find themselves repeatedly failing to understand the will of God . . . [therefore] there can be no place for smugness or dogmatism. . . . If our sensibilities are formed by this narrative, we will learn not to take ourselves too seriously; we will be very self-critical and receptive to unexpected manifestations of God's love and power.[53]

When you see how John and James respond, and you realize how hard it is for anybody to take in the magnitude of what the cross really means, you will be on your way to attaining the gift of humility. At some level, your normal assumptions, your pride and your egotistical way of thinking, are blinding you to the truth. One prime example of this is worry. Naturally, if you love people, you're going to worry about them. But do you know where constant worry comes from? It's rooted in an arrogance that assumes, *I know the way my life has to go, and God's not getting it right.* Real humility means to relax. Real humility means to laugh at yourself. Real humility means to be self-critical. The cross brings that kind of humility into our lives. When Jesus sees that his followers still don't get what he came to do, he gathers them and says, "You know that those who are regarded as rulers of the Gentiles lord it over them, and their high officials exercise authority over them. Not so with you." Jesus is talking about how most people try to influence society, to get their way. They lord it over others. They seek power and control. If I have the power, if I have the wealth, the connections, then I can get my way.

When Jesus says "Not so with you," what do you think he means? Is he saying we must withdraw and have nothing to do with society? No. Actually the principle that he's laying out rather explicitly here was already laid out earlier, in the book of the prophet Jeremiah in chapter 29. The Israelite nation had been destroyed by the Babylonian empire, and many of the people had been taken by force to Babylon. What was their attitude supposed to be toward Babylonian society, in which they were exiles? They could have tried to just keep to themselves and have nothing to do with it. Or they could have tried to infiltrate Babylon and use guerrilla tactics to take power. But what did God say to them? In Jeremiah 29:7, God said, "Seek the peace and prosperity of the city to which I have carried you into exile. Pray to the LORD for it, because if it prospers, you too will prosper." That is, I want you to seek the prosperity of Babylon. I want you to make it a great city to live in. I want you to serve your neighbors—even though their language is different and they don't believe what you believe. And I don't want you to do this merely out of a sense of duty. "Pray for it" is another way of saying "love it." Love that city, pray for it, seek to make it a prosperous, peaceful city, the greatest place to live. If Babylon prospers through your service to it, you prosper, too.

"For you," God says, "the route to gaining influence is not

taking power. Influence gained through power and control doesn't really change society; it doesn't change hearts. I'm calling you to a totally different approach. Be so sacrificially loving that the people around you, who don't believe what you believe, will soon be unable to imagine the place without you. They'll trust you because they see that you're not only out for yourself, but out for them, too. When they voluntarily begin to look up to you because of the attractiveness of your service and love, you'll have real influence. It will be an influence given to you by others, not taken by you from others." Who is the model for that way of gaining influence? It's Jesus himself, of course. How did he respond to his enemies? He didn't call down legions of angels to fight them. He died for their sins, and as he was dying he prayed for them. And if at the very heart of your worldview is a man dying for his enemies, then the way you're going to win influence in society is through service rather than power and control.

Which may be more difficult than it looks. On January 7, 2007, the *New York Times Magazine* ran an interesting article called "Happiness 101." It described *positive psychology*, a branch of psychology that seeks to take a scientific, empirical approach to what makes people happy. Researchers in this field have found that if you focus on doing and getting things that give you pleasure, it does not lead to happiness but produces what one researcher has dubbed "the hedonic treadmill." You become addicted to pleasure, and your need for the pleasure fix keeps growing: You have to do more and more. You're never satisfied, never really happy. According to the article, scientific studies have shown that the best way to increase your happiness is actually to do acts of selfless kindness, to pour yourself out for needy people. The main researcher's goal was to show that "there are ways of living that (research shows) lead to better outcomes." Some of these better outcomes were "close relationships and love," "well-being," and "meaning and purpose in life."

The researcher pointed out that when you are leading an unselfish life of service to other people, it gives you a sense of meaning, of being useful and valuable, of having a life of significance. So naturally, he argued that you should live this way in order to achieve these "better outcomes." In other words, he is saying, live a selfless life because it will make you happy—not because you ought to, or because it is moral to do so. In fact, the researcher said, "I never use the word *morality*."

But you see, if I lead an unselfish life primarily to make myself happy, then I'm *not* leading an unselfish life. I'm not doing these acts of kindness for others; I'm ultimately doing them for myself. We are being encouraged, then, to live unselfish lives for selfish reasons, which doesn't make sense.

So perhaps we should respond that the only way to live an unselfish life is to try to be moral people. But this doesn't produce true unselfishness either. Several weeks before the "Happiness 101" article, the *New York Times Magazine* had published a piece by bioethicist Peter Singer about why billionaires ought to give their money away, and it included a section about "the religious impulse." Singer noted that religious people give their money away because they feel they ought to, because then God will bless them and they'll go to heaven. I did not agree with much of the article, but I liked that he pointed out that *this is selfish*. When you decide to give away your money to meet the needs of the poor so that you can go to heaven, you're caught in the same paradox that the positive-psychology people are caught in. You want to be unselfish because there are benefits to you—in this case eternal benefits. But again, you are trying to live an unselfish life for selfish reasons, which will never work.

The preacher and theologian Jonathan Edwards, in his book *The Nature of True Virtue*, addressed this a long time before Peter Singer. If you don't believe the gospel of grace, says Edwards, if you believe you're saved by your works, then you've never done anything for the love of others or for the sheer beauty of it; you've done it for yourself. You haven't helped the proverbial little old lady across the street just for her sake—or in the end, for God's sake. You've done it because then you can look at yourself in the mirror and know that you're the kind of person who helps little old ladies across the street and you expect to go to heaven someday because of it. It's all selfish; it will become drudgery, yet you'll believe yourself superior to others.

How can we escape this self-referential trap and truly become unselfish? If secularism, psychology, and relativism on the one hand and religion and moralism on the other don't actually give us what we need to be unselfish, what does? The answer is, we need to look somewhere else besides ourselves. We need to look at Jesus. If he is indeed a substitutionary sacrifice, if he has paid for our sins, if he has proved to our insecure, skittish little hearts that we are worth everything to him, then we have everything we need in him. It's all a gift to us by grace. We don't do good things in order to connect to God or to feel better about ourselves. What a meager upgrade to our self-image these good deeds would bring, compared with what we receive from understanding why Jesus died for us and how much he loves us. If you really understand the cross, you are blasted out into the world in joyful humility. Now you do not *need* to help people, but you *want* to help them, to resemble the One who did so much for you, to bring him delight. Whether you think they are worthy of your service doesn't come into it. Only the gospel gives you a motivation for unselfish living that doesn't rob you of the benefits of unselfishness even as you enact it.

Count Nicholas von Zinzendorf, a German nobleman who was born into great power and privilege and lived from 1700 to 1760, was one of the founders of the Moravian Church. Over the years he spent his wealth down to practically zero doing good deeds, pouring himself out for others. Why? What happened that motivated him so radically? As a young man of nineteen, he was sent to visit the capital cities of Europe in order to complete his education. One day he found himself in the art gallery of Düsseldorf gazing at Domenico Feti's *Ecce homo*, a portrait of Jesus wearing a crown of thorns.[54] This image of the suffering Lord was very moving to Zinzendorf. Underneath the painting the artist had penned an inscription, words that Jesus might say to any one of us: "All this I did for thee; what doest thou for me?"

THIRTEEN

THE TEMPLE

As they approached Jerusalem and came to Bethphage and Bethany at the Mount of Olives, Jesus sent two of his disciples, saying to them, "Go to the village ahead of you, and just as you enter it, you will find a colt tied there, which no one has ever ridden. Untie it and bring it here. If anyone asks you, 'Why are you doing this?' tell him, 'The Lord needs it and will send it back here shortly.'" They went and found a colt outside in the street, tied at a doorway. As they untied it, some people standing there asked, "What are you doing, untying that colt?" They answered as Jesus had told them to, and the people let them go. When they brought the colt to Jesus and threw their cloaks over it, he sat on it. Many people spread their cloaks on the road, while others spread branches they had cut in the fields. Those who went ahead and those who followed shouted, "Hosanna!" "Blessed is he who comes in the name of the Lord!" "Blessed is the

coming kingdom of our father David!" "Hosanna in the
highest!"

(Mark 11:1–10)

When Jesus rode into Jerusalem, people laid down their cloaks on the road in front of him and hailed him as a king coming in the name of the house of David. This type of parade was culturally appropriate in that era: A king would ride into town publicly and be hailed by cheering crowds. But Jesus deliberately departed from the script and did something very different. He didn't ride in on a powerful war horse the way a king would; he was mounted on a *polos*, that is, a colt or a small donkey. Here was Jesus Christ, the King of authoritative, miraculous power, riding into town on a steed fit for a child or a hobbit. In this way, Jesus let it be known that he was the One prophesied in Zechariah, the great Messiah to come:

Rejoice greatly, O Daughter of Zion! Shout, Daughter
of Jerusalem! See, your King comes to you, righteous and
having salvation, gentle and riding on a donkey, on a colt,
the foal of a donkey.

(Zechariah 9:9)

This odd juxtaposition demonstrates that Jesus was King, but that he didn't fit into the world's categories of kingship. He brought together majesty and meekness. One of the greatest sermons ever written and preached in 1738 by Jonathan Edwards, titled "The Excellency of Christ." Edwards's imagination was captured by the prophetic vision of Jesus's disciple John in Revelation 5:5–6: "Then one of the elders said to me, 'Do not weep! See, the Lion of the tribe of Judah, the Root of David, has triumphed. He is able to open the scroll and its seven seals.'

Then I saw a Lamb, looking as if it had been slain, standing in the center of the throne." John is told to look for a lion, but there in the midst of the throne is a lamb. Edwards meditates on this:

> The lion excels in strength and in the majesty of his appearance and voice. The lamb excels in meekness and patience . . . is [sacrificed] for food . . . and . . . clothing. But we see that Christ is in the text compared to both, because the diverse excellencies of both wonderfully meet in him. . . . There is in Jesus Christ . . . a conjunction of such really diverse excellencies as otherwise would have seemed to us utterly incompatible in the same subject. . . .[55]

Edwards goes on to list in detail all the ways that Jesus combines character traits that we would consider mutually exclusive. In Jesus we find infinite majesty yet complete humility, perfect justice yet boundless grace, absolute sovereignty yet utter submission, all-sufficiency in himself yet entire trust and dependence on God.

But in Jesus the result of these extremes of character is not mental and emotional breakdown. Jesus's personality is a complete and beautiful whole. Watch this mighty King ride a little donkey into Jerusalem and deal with what he finds there.

Opening the Temple

When Jesus arrived at Jerusalem, he went to the temple, and things got a little bit more complicated. Mark writes:

> *Jesus entered Jerusalem and went to the temple. He looked around at everything, but since it was already late, he*

*went out to Bethany with the Twelve. The next day . . .
on reaching Jerusalem, Jesus entered the temple area
and began driving out those who were buying and selling there. He overturned the tables of the money changers and the benches of those selling doves, and would not
allow anyone to carry merchandise through the temple
courts. And as he taught them, he said, "Is it not written:
'My house will be called a house of prayer for all nations'?
But you have made it a den of robbers." The chief priests
and the teachers of the law heard this and began looking
for a way to kill him, for they feared him, because the
whole crowd was amazed at his teaching.*

(Mark 11:11–12, 15–18)

Mark mentions that Jesus "entered the temple area." Why is
that significant? When you stepped inside the temple door, the
first area you got to was the court of the Gentiles—the *ethne* or
"nations." This was the only part where non-Jews were allowed. It
was the biggest section of the temple, and you had to go through
it to get to the rest. All the business operations of the temple were
set up there. And what an operation it was! When Jesus walked
in, he would immediately have seen great throngs of people buying and selling animals at dozens of stalls and exchanging for-
eign currencies at money changers' tables. Thousands of people
flooded into Jerusalem bringing and buying tens of thousands
of animals to be sacrificed. The ancient historian Josephus tells
us that in Passover week one year, 255,000 lambs were bought,
sold, and sacrificed in the temple courts.[56] Think of how tumul-
tuous, loud, and confusing our financial trading floors are—and
then add livestock. And this was the place where the Gentiles
were supposed to find God through quiet reflection and prayer.

Jesus's reaction to all this was to start throwing the furniture over. Imagine the leaders hurrying to him in panic: "What's going on? Why are you doing this?" He quoted from the prophet Isaiah in reply: "My house will be called a house of prayer for all nations"—that is, for the Gentiles. We are told this amazed those who heard him. Why? For one thing, it was popularly believed that when the Messiah showed up he would purge the temple of foreigners. Instead, here is Jesus clearing the temple *for* the Gentiles—acting as their advocate.[57] In our multicultural society it's easy to like that about Jesus. But what he was doing was even more subversive. Jesus was challenging the sacrificial system altogether and saying that the Gentiles—the pagan, unwashed Gentiles—could now go directly to God in prayer. This was amazing because the people knew the history of the tabernacle and the temple.

The story of the temple starts all the way back in the Garden of Eden. That primal garden was a sanctuary; it was the place where the presence of God dwelled. It was a paradise, because death, deformity, evil, and imperfection cannot coexist with God's presence. In the presence of God there is *shalom*, absolute flourishing, fulfillment, joy, and bliss. But when the first human beings decided to build their lives on other things besides God, to let other things besides God give them their ultimate meaning and significance, paradise was lost. As Adam and Eve were banished from the sanctuary of God, they turned around and saw "a flaming sword flashing back and forth" (Genesis 3:24). No one could ever get past this flaming sword that barred the way back into the presence of God.

Turning from God has had dreadful consequences. Building our lives on other things—on power, status, acclaim, family, race, nationality—has caused conflicts, wars, violence, poverty, disease, and death. We've trampled one another; we've trampled on this earth. That means it's not enough just to say, "Sorry, may I please get back into the presence of God?" If you've been the victim of a heinous crime, if you have suffered violence, and the perpetrator (or even the judge) says, "Sorry, can't we just let it go?" you would say, "No, that would be an injustice." Your refusal would rightly have nothing to do with bitterness or vengeance. If you have been badly wronged, you know that saying sorry is not enough. Something else is required—some kind of costly payment must be made to put things right.

The flaming sword is the sword of eternal justice, and it will not fail to exact payment. Nobody can get back into the presence of God unless they go under the sword, unless they pay for the wrong that has been done. But who could survive the sword? No one. And if no one can survive the sword, then how will we ever get back into the presence of God?

These questions remained in spite of the fact that God established a provisional solution for his chosen people, the Israelites: first through the tabernacle and then the temple.[58] In the middle of the temple was the holy of holies. It was a small space, covered by a thick veil to shield people from the *shekinah* presence of God. Remember, God's immediate presence was fatal to human beings. Just once a year, on Yom Kippur, the Day of Atonement, the high priest could go inside briefly, but only if he carried a blood sacrifice. Why? Because there was no way back into the presence of God without going under the sword. Even then the blood sacrifice was only inadequately symbolic of the true atoning work that had to happen. What's more, it didn't extend access to the rest of us—those not part of the Jewish people. The tabernacle, the temple, and the whole sacrificial system—the only solution to the problem of the sword and the only access, however limited, to the presence of God—were only for the Israelites. So when Jesus quoted Isaiah to imply that the Gentiles could get access to the presence of God, the people were amazed.

Yet the prophets kept promising that someday the glory of God would cover the earth as the waters fill the sea—in other words, the whole world would become a holy of holies. The whole earth would be filled with the glory and presence of God again. And people from all nations, races, backgrounds, and social classes would be welcome in that presence.

Beautiful prophesies. But still: How would they get past the sword?

The answer had been in the book of Isaiah, though most people didn't see it. Isaiah 53:8 says about the Messiah: "He will be *cut off* from the land of the living." And in Revelation, when John looks at the throne, the place of ultimate power in the universe, why does he see a slaughtered lamb? Because the death of Jesus Christ—the Lamb of God—is the greatest royal triumph in the history of the cosmos. When Jesus went under the sword, it broke his body, but it also broke itself. This was what one author famously called "the death of Death in the death of Christ."[59] Jesus took the sword for you and me. That's why at the moment Jesus died, the veil that covered the holy of holies was ripped from top to bottom (Mark 15:38). It wasn't just ruined; it was made obsolete, so that now we all have access to the presence of God. The flaming sword claimed its victim; the veil was parted; and the way back into the garden was permanently reopened.

The people may have been startled by Jesus's display of controlled, authoritative, righteous anger in overturning the tables in the temple. But what absolutely shocked them is that he was overturning the sacrificial system of the temple and opening the way into the presence of God for everyone.

Clearing the Temple

Jesus actually visited the temple twice. He went there briefly upon his arrival in Jerusalem, then stayed that night with his disciples in Bethany, a couple of miles outside the city. The next day they came back into Jerusalem to visit the temple again (this is when Jesus overturned the tables), and on their way into the city, Mark records the following story:

> *The next day as they were leaving Bethany, Jesus was hungry. Seeing in the distance a fig tree in leaf, he went to find out if it had any fruit. When he reached it, he found nothing but leaves, because it was not the season for figs. Then he said to the tree, "May no one ever eat fruit from you again." And his disciples heard him say it.*
>
> (Mark 11:12–14)

I must say, on the surface it looks very bad for Jesus. A lot of people have had trouble with Jesus's reaction to the fig tree. Putting a curse on a tree because it was not bearing fruit, and out of season, no less? It seems petulant and mean. But let's look at this closely. This is no fit of temper.

Middle Eastern fig trees bore two kinds of fruit. As the leaves were starting to come in the spring, before the figs came, the branches bore little nodules, which were abundant and very good to eat. Travelers liked to pick them off and eat them as they made their journey. If you found a fig tree that had begun to sprout leaves but had none of these delicious nodules, you would know that something was wrong. It might look okay from a distance because the leaves had emerged, but if it had no nodules it was diseased or maybe even dying inside. Growth without fruit was a sign of decay. Jesus is simply pronouncing that such is the case here. Remember that this happens between his first arrival at the temple and his return to the temple the next day. Jesus seizes the opportunity to provide a private, memorable object lesson, a parable against hollow religiosity, with the fig tree as a visual aid.

So what is the lesson about? Jesus finds the fig tree not doing its appointed job. The tree became a perfect metaphor for Israel, and beyond that, for those claiming to be God's people but who do not bear fruit for him. Jesus was returning to a place that was religiously very busy, just like most churches are: tasks, committees, noise, people coming and going, lots of transactions. But the busyness contained no spirituality. Nobody was actually praying. There are many things we do that can appear to be signs of real belief but can grow without real heart change. Evidently we can be very busy in church activities without real heart change and without real compassionate involvement with others.

Later that day, Jesus would clear the temple of all that fruitless activity. He would take the private object lesson of the fig tree and turn it into a necessary public spectacle. Jesus is saying that he wants more than busyness; he wants the kind of character change that only comes from realizing that you have been ransomed. If you're an anxious or impatient person, is it clear to everybody around that you are overcoming that? Do you have the power to wait through Jesus's delays? If you're an angry or unforgiving person, have you clearly begun to conquer anger? Are you learning to absorb the cost of forgiveness? If you're a fearful person, a self-hating person, or a self-aggrandizing person, is it very clear to the people who know you best that your character is undergoing radical regeneration? Or are you just very busy with religious activities?

At the end of Jonathan Edwards's sermon on the paradoxical character of Jesus, he says that these same radically different traits that are normally never combined in any one person *will be reproduced in you because you are in the presence of Jesus Christ.* You're not just becoming a nicer person or a more disciplined person or a more moral person. The life and character of Jesus—the King who ambles into Jerusalem on a donkey, then storms into the temple with the audacity to say "This is my house"—are being reproduced in you. You're becoming a more complete person, the person you were designed to be. The person you were ransomed to be.

There is a final irony to all of this. Jesus, who unites such apparent extremes of character into such an integrated and balanced whole, demands an extreme response from every one of us. He forces our hand at every turn in the story. This man who throws open the gates of his kingdom to everyone, then warns the most devout insiders that their standing in the kingdom is in jeopardy without fruitfulness, is forever closing down our options. This man who can be weakened by a touch in a crowd on his way to bring a little girl back from the dead is a man you dare not tear your eyes from. (And we haven't even yet witnessed the true depths of his restraint or the heights of his power.)

He is both the rest and the storm, both the victim and the wielder of the flaming sword, and you must accept him or reject him on the basis of both. Either you'll have to kill him or you'll have to crown him. The one thing you can't do is just say, "What an interesting guy." Those teachers of the law who began plotting to kill Jesus at the end of this episode in the temple—they may have been dead wrong about him, but their reaction makes perfect sense.

Please don't try to keep Jesus on the periphery of your life. He cannot remain there. Give yourself to him—center your entire life on him—and let his power reproduce his character in you.

FOURTEEN

THE FEAST

For the ancient Jews—and still for Jews today—Passover was an annual meal that commemorated a defining moment in the history of Israel. More than a millennium before the time of Jesus, the Israelites had been enslaved to Egypt's pharaoh, trapped in miserable bondage. After sending many plagues to Egypt to loosen the pharaoh's oppressive grip on Israel, one night God sent the final plague; he unsheathed the sword of divine justice. And this justice would fall on *everyone*. It could not "pass over" the Jews simply because they were Jews. In every home in Egypt—of Jews and Egyptians alike—someone would die under the wrath of justice. The only way for your family to escape was to put your faith in God's sacrificial provision; namely, you had to slay a lamb and put the blood on the doors as a sign of your faith in God. In every home that night there would either be a dead child or a dead lamb. When justice came down, either it fell on your family or you took shelter under the substitute, under the blood of the lamb. If you did accept this shelter, then death passed over you and you were saved; that's why it was called Passover. You were saved only on the basis of faith in a substitutionary sacrifice.

This is how God delivered the Israelites and led them into freedom, into the Promised Land. Every year the Passover meal commemorated this deliverance (referred to as the exodus), which had been the most important moment in the life of Israel as a nation and as a people.

But as dramatic and moving as this deliverance was, it leaves us with a nagging question. *Why in the world would the sacrifice of a woolly little quadruped exempt you from justice?* The answer lies in what happens when Jesus and his disciples celebrate Passover. Mark writes:

> *On the first day of the Feast of Unleavened Bread, when it was customary to sacrifice the Passover lamb, Jesus' disciples asked him, "Where do you want us to go and make preparations for you to eat the Passover?" So he sent two of his disciples, telling them, "Go into the city, and a man carrying a jar of water will meet you. Follow him. Say to the owner of the house he enters, 'The Teacher asks: Where is my guest room, where I may eat the Passover with my disciples?' He will show you a large upper room, furnished and ready. Make preparations for us there." The disciples left, went into the city and found things just as Jesus had told them. So they prepared the Passover.*
>
> (Mark 14:12–16)

The Passover meal had to be prepared in a certain way and had a distinct form. It included four points at which the presider, holding a glass of wine, got up and explained the feast's meaning. The four cups of wine represented the four promises made by God in Exodus 6:6–7. These promises were for rescue from

Egypt, for freedom from slavery, for redemption by God's divine power, and for a renewed relationship with God. The third cup came at a point when the meal was almost completely eaten. The presider would use words from Deuteronomy 26 to bless the elements—the bread, the herbs, the lamb—by explaining how they were symbolic reminders of various aspects of the early Israelites' captivity and deliverance. For example, he would show them the bread and say, "This is the bread of our affliction, which our fathers ate in the wilderness."

Jesus was the presider at this Passover meal with the disciples, and Mark recounts what happened when Jesus raised the third cup:

> *While they were eating, Jesus took bread, gave thanks and broke it, and gave it to his disciples, saying, "Take it; this is my body." Then he took the cup, gave thanks and offered it to them, and they all drank from it. "This is my blood of the covenant, which is poured out for many," he said to them. "I tell you the truth, I will not drink again of the fruit of the vine until that day when I drink it anew in the kingdom of God."*
>
> (Mark 14:22–25)

Imagine the astonishment of the disciples when, blessing the elements and explaining their symbolism, Jesus departs from the script that has been reenacted by generation after generation. He shows them the bread and says, "This is my body." What does that mean? Jesus is saying, "This is the bread of *my* affliction, the bread of *my* suffering, because I'm going to lead the ultimate exodus and bring you the ultimate deliverance from bondage."

In ancient times when someone would say, "I'm not going to eat or drink until I _____," they were making an oath. For example, in Acts 23, some people get so mad at Paul that they say they're not going to eat or drink until they kill him. It's like when we say, "I'm going to do this if it kills me," but in biblical times this was an oath that was taken very seriously and was literally marked with blood. This oath meant you were making a covenant—a solemn relationship of obligation—between you and another party. Like signing a contract. But this covenant was established and sealed by killing an animal, cutting it in half, and walking between the pieces as you stated your oath. Or sometimes you would spill the blood and have it sprinkled on you as you made your promise. It's gory and repulsive to us, but it was a way of saying, "If I do not fulfill my promise, may my blood be spilled, may I be cut in half." This was a very vivid way of making the covenant binding. Remember what Jesus said when he took the cup:

> *Then he took the cup, gave thanks and offered it to them, and they all drank from it. "This is my blood of the covenant, which is poured out for many," he said to them. "I tell you the truth, I will not drink again of the fruit of the vine until that day when I drink it anew in the kingdom of God."*
>
> (Mark 14:23–25)

Jesus's words mean that as a result of his substitutionary sacrifice there is now a new covenant between God and us. And the basis of this relationship is Jesus's own blood: "my blood of the covenant." When he announces that he will not eat or drink until he meets us in the kingdom of God, Jesus is promising that he is unconditionally committed to us: "I am going to bring you into the Father's arms. I'm going to bring you to the feast of the King." Jesus often compares God's kingdom to sitting at a big feast. In Matthew 8, Jesus says, "I say to you that many will come from the east and the west, and will take their places at the feast . . . in the kingdom of heaven." Jesus promises that we will be at this kingdom feast with him.

With these simple gestures of holding up the bread and the wine, with the simple words "This is my body . . . this is my blood," Jesus is saying that all the earlier deliverances, the earlier sacrifices, the lambs at Passover, were pointing to himself. Just as the first Passover was observed the night before God redeemed the Israelites from slavery through the blood of the lambs, this Passover meal was eaten the night before God redeemed the world from sin and death through the blood of Jesus.

The Main Course

Jesus's last meal with his disciples departed from the script in another way too. When Jesus stood up to bless the food, he held up bread. All Passover meals had bread. He blessed the wine—all Passover meals had wine. But not one of the Gospels mentions a main course. There is no mention of lamb at this Passover meal. Passover was not a vegetarian meal, of course. What kind of Passover would be celebrated without lamb? There was no lamb *on* the table because the Lamb of God was *at* the table. Jesus was the main course. That's the reason that when John the Baptist saw Jesus for the first time, he said, "Look, the Lamb of God, who takes away the sin of the world!" (John 1:29). It is also why in Isaiah 53, the prophet writes about the Messiah:

> *The LORD has laid on him the iniquity of us all. . . .*
> *He was oppressed and afflicted, yet he did not open*
> *his mouth; he was led like a lamb to the slaughter. . . .*

he poured out his life unto death, and was numbered
with the transgressors.

(Isaiah 53:6–7, 12)

In Mark, when Jesus says, "This is my body. . . . This is my blood . . . poured out," he means: *I'm the One that Isaiah and John spoke about. I am the Lamb of God to which all the other lambs pointed, the Lamb that takes away the sin of the world.*

On the cross Jesus got what *we* deserved: The sin, guilt, and brokenness of the world fell upon him. He loved us so much he took divine justice on himself so that we could be passed over, forever.

It bears repeating: All love, all real, life-changing love, is substitutionary sacrifice. You have never loved a broken person, you have never loved a guilty person, you have never loved a hurting person except through substitutionary sacrifice. Two chapters back I gave a couple of examples; here are a few more.

Say you're one of the cool kids in high school, and there's a classmate who is considered geeky. Nobody likes her; she's isolated and alienated. You try to reach out and be her friend. The next thing you know, the other cool kids are coming to you and saying, "What are you doing with *her?*" What's happening is, some of that geekiness is rubbing off on you. You're not so cool anymore if you hang out with her. There is no way for you to diminish her isolation without entering into it, without some of it falling on you.

One more example: I read some years ago in *National Geographic* that after a forest fire in Yellowstone National Park, some forest rangers began a trek up a mountain to survey the damage. One ranger found a bird of which nothing was left but the carbonized, petrified shell, covered in ashes, huddled at the base of a tree. Somewhat sickened by this eerie sight, the ranger knocked the bird over with a stick—and three tiny chicks scurried out from under their dead mother's wings. When the blaze had arrived, the mother had remained steadfast instead of running. Because she had been willing to die, those under the cover of her wings lived. And Jesus said, "Jerusalem, Jerusalem, you that kill the prophets and stone those sent to you, how often I have longed to gather your children together, as a hen gathers her chicks under her wings" (Luke 13:34). He did indeed gather Jerusalem's children under his wings—and he was consumed. All real, life-changing love is costly, substitutionary sacrifice.

The Last Course

When Luke describes this same meal in his story of Jesus, he records a few more of Jesus's words. Luke adds:

> *And he took bread, gave thanks and broke it, and gave it to them, saying, "This is my body given for you; do this in remembrance of me."*
>
> (Luke 22:19)

Jesus is saying that in remembrance of him, the disciples and anyone who believes in him are to eat the bread and drink the cup together. This practice is called the "Lord's Supper" (1 Corinthians 11:20) for obvious reasons, but it is also called the "Lord's table" (1 Corinthians 10:21), "communion," "cup of blessing" (1 Corinthians 10:16), and "breaking of bread" (Acts 2:42). The bread that is broken, given, and eaten in the Lord's Supper is a reminder of Christ's body given and broken on the cross for our sins. The wine poured out to drink is a reminder of Christ's blood poured out on the cross for our sins. So when anyone eats that bread and drinks that wine they are reminded of the sacrificial, substitutionary love of Jesus.

The first Passover meal in Egypt was, of course, an actual meal. It was not enough that a lamb was slain and its blood put on the doorposts. The lamb also had to be eaten; it had to be taken in. In the same way, the Lord's Supper is a way of "taking in" the death of Christ for yourself and appropriating it personally. Mark writes:

> *While they were eating, Jesus took bread, gave thanks and broke it, and gave it to his disciples, saying, "Take it; this is my body."*
>
> (Mark 14:22)

Jesus says, "Take it." He lets us know that we have to *take* what he is doing for us. We have to receive it actively. It is common to distribute the Lord's Supper and say, "Feed on him in your hearts by faith." You don't get the benefit of food unless you take it in and digest it. You can have a meal piled high in front of you, all the food cooked to perfection, and you could still starve to death. To be nourished by a meal, you have to *eat it*. The excellent preparation of the food doesn't help you if you're not willing to pick it up and take it into yourself. Taking it is the same as saying, "This is the real food I need—Christ's unconditional commitment to me."

The "mealness" of the Lord's Supper is a reminder that no one can appropriate the benefits of Jesus's death unless he calls them into a personal relationship with him. To share a meal with someone—particularly in Jesus's place and time—is to have a relationship. So Jesus is saying that we need a personal relationship with him if all the benefits of his perfect, substitutionary, sacrificial suffering are to come to us.

The "mealness" also tells us something else. The Jews celebrated each Passover by eating the feast with their families. The Passover is a family meal. Then why was Jesus pulling his disciples out of their families and organizing a Passover meal with them? Because he was creating an altogether new family. When you have been raised with brothers and sisters, you share a powerful bond. You have been through everything with them; you have more common experiences with them than with anyone else. Earlier Jesus had said, "Whoever does God's will is my brother and sister and mother" (Mark 3:35). As one writer put it: "What binds [Christians] together is not common education, common race, common income levels, common politics, common nationality, common accents, common jobs, or anything else of that sort. Christians come together . . . because they have been saved by Jesus Christ. . . . They are a band of natural enemies who love one another for Jesus's sake."[60] When you take the Lord's Supper, you are doing it with brothers and sisters, with family. This bond is so life-transforming that it creates a basis for unity as strong as if people had been raised together.

Finally, the Lord's Supper does something more beautiful yet: It points toward our future with Jesus. As he presides over the Passover with his disciples, he tells them the rest of the story of the world in two sentences: "This is my blood of the covenant, which is poured out for many . . . I tell you the truth, I will not drink again of the fruit of the vine until that day when I drink it anew in the kingdom of God." He is saying that this Passover meal makes the ultimate feast possible, and in so doing, draws an inexorable arc between the events of the ensuing three days and their consummation in the future.

Jesus's words call to mind some of the stunning prophecies about the future kingdom. Psalm 96:12–13 says, "All the trees of the forest will sing for joy; they will sing before the LORD, for he comes, he comes to judge the earth." Isaiah 55:12 says, "The mountains and the hills will burst into song before you, and all the trees of the field will clap their hands."

If you put seeds into a pot of soil and then put it away in the dark, away from the sun, the seeds go into dormancy. They can't grow to their potential. But if you bring the pot with seeds into the presence of the sun, all that has been locked within them bursts forth. The Bible says that everything in this world—not just we human beings but even the plants, the trees, the rocks—is dormant. These things are just shadows of what they have been, would be, and will be in the presence of their Creator. When the Lamb of God presides over the final feast and the presence of God covers the earth again, the trees and the hills will clap and dance, so alive will they be. And if trees and hills will be able to clap and dance in the future kingdom, picture what you and I will be able to do.

The Lord's Supper gives us a small, but very real, foretaste of that future.

Imagine you were in Egypt just after that first Passover. If you stopped Israelites in those days and said, "Who are you and what is happening here?" they would say, "I was a slave, under a sentence of death, but I took shelter under the blood of the lamb and escaped that bondage, and now God lives in our midst and we are following him to the Promised Land." That is exactly what Christians say today. If you trust in Jesus's substitutionary sacrifice, the greatest longings of your heart will be satisfied on the day you sit down for that eternal feast in the promised kingdom of God.

FIFTEEN

THE CUP

The Greeks and Romans have left us many stories of leaders and heroes as they faced death, and without exception these people were calm and dispassionate in their final hours. Think of Socrates, who was condemned to drink hemlock as a means of execution. The story of his demise has him surrounded by his followers, coolly tossing off ironic one-liners. By contrast, in Jewish literature such as in 1 and 2 Maccabees, you'll see that when Jews wrote accounts of the deaths of major figures and heroes they did not make them cool and removed like the Greeks; rather, they are shown as hot-blooded and fearless, and they praise God as they are being sliced to pieces by their persecutors. Nothing in either of these traditions—indeed nothing in ancient literature— resembles the portrayal that Mark gives us of Jesus's final hours as he faced his death. Mark records:

They went to a place called Gethsemane, and Jesus said
to his disciples, "Sit here while I pray." He took Peter,

James, and John along with him, and he began to be
deeply distressed and troubled. "My soul is overwhelmed
with sorrow to the point of death," he said to them. "Stay
here and keep watch." Going a little farther, he fell to the
ground and prayed that if possible the hour might pass
from him. "Abba, Father," he said, "everything is possible
for you. Take this cup from me. Yet not what I will, but
what you will."

(Mark 14:32–36)

Here Jesus, just before his execution, opens his heart to his disciples, opens his heart to God, opens his heart to the readers of Mark's Gospel, and lays bare his struggles, his agony, his fears about facing death. He turns to God and pleads, "Is there a way this cup can be taken from me? Is there any way I can be let off the hook? Is there any way I can get out of this mission?" Up to this point Jesus has been completely in control. Nothing seems to have surprised him so far. Jesus always knows what's going on: Nothing seems to jar him. But all of a sudden we read that "he began to be deeply distressed." The Greek word translated "deeply distressed" actually means "astonished." Think back on the Gospel of Mark up to this point. Jesus has been totally unflappable. But here, suddenly, something he sees, something he realizes, something he experiences, stuns the eternal Son of God.

Jesus is also, according to the text, "troubled." The Greek verb here means "to be overcome with horror." Imagine you're walking down a street, you turn a corner, and there in front of you is someone you love, mutilated in a terrible car accident. What do you feel? Nausea. Your horror is like a physical cloud rising up to choke you. That emotion is what Jesus is experiencing. He says so: "My soul is overwhelmed with sorrow to the point of death."

Jesus's struggle is not only unique in ancient accounts of the death of prominent figures, but it is also almost unique in *church* history. That's strange, isn't it? We have many true accounts of Christian men and women being killed for their faith—thrown to wild animals, cut to pieces, burned at the stake. It appears that many of them faced their deaths more calmly than Jesus did. Take Polycarp, bishop of Smyrna, an early Christian leader. Near the end of his life, he was taken before a magistrate and told that he would be burned at the stake. The magistrate said, in effect, "I will give you one more chance: You can reject Christianity, you can recant, and avoid execution." Some witnesses wrote down Polycarp's reply: "The fire you threaten burns but an hour and is quenched after a little. . . . You do not know the fire of the coming judgment. . . . But why do you delay? Come, do what you will."[61]

Or take Nicholas Ridley and Hugh Latimer, who were burned at the stake for their faith in Oxford, England, in 1555. They were tied side by side, and when the fire was lit at their feet, Latimer said: "Be of good comfort Master Ridley, and play the man: we shall this day light such a candle by God's grace in England, as I trust shall never be put out."[62]

Why is it that many of Jesus's followers have died "better" than Jesus? Of course, he must have been facing something that Polycarp, Ridley, and Latimer were not facing, something that none of the other martyrs were facing.

Something happened in the garden—Jesus saw, felt, sensed something—and it shocked the unshockable Son of God. What was it? He was facing something beyond physical torment, even beyond physical death—something so much worse that these were like flea bites by comparison. He was smothered by a mere whiff of what he would go through on the cross. Didn't he know he was going to die? Yes, but we're not talking about information here. Of course he knew that; he had told the disciples so repeatedly. But now he is beginning to *taste* what he will experience on the cross, and it goes far beyond physical torture and death. What is this terrible thing? It's at the very heart of Jesus's prayer here. He says, "Take this cup from me."

Remember that in the Hebrew Scriptures, "the cup" is a metaphor for the wrath of God on human evil. It's an image of divine justice poured out on injustice. For example, in Ezekiel 23:32–34, we read, "You will drink . . . a cup large and deep; . . . the cup of ruin and desolation, . . . and tear your breasts." Similarly, in Isaiah 51:22, God speaks of "the cup that made you stagger; . . . the goblet of my wrath." All his life, because of Jesus's eternal dance with his Father and the Spirit, whenever he turned to the Father, the Spirit flooded him with love. What happened visibly and audibly at Jesus's baptism and at his transfiguration happened invisibly, inaudibly, every time he prayed. But in the garden of Gethsemane, he turns to the Father and all he can see before him is wrath, the abyss, the chasm, the nothingness of the cup. God is the source of all love, all life, all light, all coherence. Therefore exclusion from God is exclusion from the source of all light, all love, all coherence. Jesus began to experience the spiritual, cosmic, infinite disintegration that would happen when he became separated from his Father on the cross. Jesus began to experience merely a foretaste of that, and he staggered.

The Wrath of Love

Here you may say, "I don't like the idea of the wrath of God. I want a God of love."

The problem is that if you want a loving God, you have to have an angry God. Please think about it. Loving people can get angry, not in spite of their love but *because* of it. In fact, the more closely and deeply you love people in your life, the angrier you can get. Have you noticed that? When you see people who are harmed or abused, you get mad. If you see people abusing themselves, you get mad at *them*, out of love. Your senses of love and justice are activated together, not in opposition to each other. If you see people destroying themselves or destroying other people and you *don't* get mad, it's because you don't care. You're too absorbed in yourself, too cynical, too hard. The more loving you are, the more ferociously angry you will be at whatever harms your beloved. And the greater the harm, the more resolute your opposition will be.

When we think of God's wrath, we usually think of God's justice, and that is right. Those who care about justice get angry when they see justice being trampled upon, and we should expect a perfectly just God to do the same. But we don't ponder how much his anger is also a function of his love and goodness. The Bible tells us that God loves everything he has made. That's one of the reasons he's angry at what's going on in his creation; he is angry at anything or anyone that is destroying the people and world he loves. His capacity for love is so much greater than ours—and the cumulative extent of evil in the world is so vast—that the word *wrath* doesn't really do justice to how God rightly feels when he looks at the world. So it makes no sense to say, "I don't want a wrathful God, I want a loving God." If God is loving and good, he must be angry at evil—angry enough to do something about it.

Consider this also: If you don't believe in a God of wrath, you have no idea of your value. Here's what I mean. A god without wrath has no need to go to the cross and suffer incredible agony and die in order to save you. Picture on the left a god who pays nothing in order to love you, and picture on the right the God of the Bible, who, because he's angry at evil, must go to the cross, absorb the debt, pay the ransom, and suffer immense torment. How do you know how much the "free love" god loves you or how valuable you are to him? Well, his love is just a concept. You don't know at all. This god pays no price in order to love you. How valuable are you to the God of the Bible? Valuable enough that he would go to these depths for you.

A correspondence between C. S. Lewis and a man named Malcolm has been collected in a book called *Letters to Malcolm: Chiefly on Prayer*. In one letter Malcolm said that he was uncomfortable with the idea that God gets angry. He found it more helpful to think of God's power and justice like a live electrical wire. He said, "The live wire doesn't feel angry with us, but if we blunder against it we get a shock." Lewis replied: "My dear Malcolm: What do you suppose you have gained by substituting the image of a live wire for that of angered majesty? You have shut us up all in despair, for the angry can forgive, but electricity can't. . . . Turn God's wrath into mere enlightened disapproval and you turn his love into mere humanitarianism. The 'consuming fire' and the 'perfect beauty' both vanish. We have, instead, a judicious headmistress or a conscientious magistrate. It comes of being high-minded. . . . Liberalizing and civilizing analogies can only lead us astray."[63] Your conception of God's love—and of your value in his sight—will only be as big as your understanding of his wrath.

The Obedience of Love

When the circumstances of life are giving you the desires of your heart, you're content. Suffering happens, we might say, when there's a gap between the desires of your heart and the circumstances of your life, and the bigger the gap, the greater the suffering. What do you do when that gap gets too wide? One response is to change the circumstances—to get off the path that's taking you into suffering. Of course, sometimes this is the right response; our present circumstances may really have to change. There may be a very unhealthy relationship that needs to be ended or put on a different course, or a medical condition that needs to be treated aggressively. We should not accept all circumstances with passive fatalism.

Many people have a pattern, however, of dealing with almost any suffering by getting out of town, breaking promises, pulling out of relationships. They invariably try to go someplace where their desires are satisfied, because they consider their desires all-important, which makes their circumstances negotiable. They are willing to do practically anything to avoid suffering. The problem is that life circumstances rarely oblige. Try that new set of circumstances and in six months you'll need another set.

The Eightfold Path of Buddhism doesn't advocate that response, and neither did the ancient Stoics; they say that always avoiding suffering has no virtue or integrity at all. To say, "When there's a gap between your desires and your circumstances, change the circumstances" violates the teachings of these and other currents of religious thought. Instead, they say, what you do need to do is suppress your desires. Get on top of them and become cool, detached, and dispassionate. Then you can keep your promises and stay on the path. The circumstances are fated, while the desires are just an illusion. That's the reason Socrates wasn't panicking at the end of his life. He didn't care to keep on living. He had succeeded in detaching himself.

Of course, there are times when we need to suppress our desires, because they're so often destructive. But to eliminate all desire is to eliminate our ability to love; and God made us to love.

When you look at Jesus here in the Garden of Gethsemane,

he appears to be taking the first approach. He's certainly not taking the way of detachment; he's pouring his heart out. He's undone. And he's honestly and desperately asking God to change the circumstances, praying "that if possible the hour might pass from him." He cries out, "Abba, Father . . . everything is possible for you. Take this cup from me." He's contending with the Father, asking him for a way out, asking for another way to rescue us without having to go personally under the flaming sword.

But look closely: He's actually not taking his circumstances into his own hands. In the end, he's obeying—relinquishing control over his circumstances and submitting his desires to the will of the Father. He says to God, "Yet not what I will, but what you will." He is wrestling but obeying in love.

It would still be possible, at this eleventh hour, for Jesus to abort his mission and leave us to perish. But he doesn't consider that as an option. He's begging the Father to carry out the mission some other way, but he doesn't ask him to abandon it altogether. Why? Because as horrible as the cup is, he knows that his immediate desire (to be spared) must bow before his ultimate one (to spare us).

Often what seem to be our deepest desires are really just our *loudest* desires. Do you know how, especially when you are in intense pain or great temptation, you just can't think straight? You turn on the people who love you. You make shockingly self-destructive decisions. You say and do things that you know are not only hurtful but actually undermine the people and values you love most.

But at one of the supreme moments of personal pain in the history of the world, Jesus doesn't do that. He says, "Yet not what I will, but what you will." He's not even saying to God, "I think you're wrong, but I'm going to let you win this one." No; he's saying, "I trust you no matter what I'm feeling right now. I know that your desires are ultimately my desires. Do what we both know must be done."

And in so doing Jesus is absolutely obedient to the will of God. *Yet not what I will, but what you will.* Jesus is subordinating his loudest desires to his deepest desires by putting them in the Father's hands. As if to say, "If the circumstances of life do not satisfy the present desires of my heart, I'm not going to suppress those desires, but I'm not going to surrender to them, either. I know that they will only be satisfied, eventually, in the Father. I will trust and obey him, put myself in his hands, and go forward."

Jesus doesn't deny his emotions, and he doesn't avoid the suffering. *He loves into the suffering.* In the midst of his suffering, he obeys for the love of the Father—and for the love of us.

And when you see that, instead of perpetually denying your desires or changing your circumstances, you'll be able to trust the Father in your suffering. You will be able to trust that because Jesus took the cup, your deepest desires and your actual circumstances are going to keep converging until they unite forever on the day of the eternal feast.

In a great sermon, "Christ's Agony," Jonathan Edwards put it like this:

> [In the Garden of Gethsemane, Jesus] had then a near view of that furnace of wrath, into which he was to be cast; he was brought to the mouth of the furnace that he might look into it, and stand and view its raging flames, and see the glowings of its heat, that he might know where he was going and what he was about to suffer. . . . There are two things that render Christ's love wonderful: 1. That he should be willing to endure sufferings that were so great; and 2. That he should be

willing to endure them to make atonement for wicked-
ness that was so great. But in order to its being properly said, Christ of his own act and choice endured
sufferings that were so great . . . [it was] necessary that
he should have an extraordinary sense how great these
sufferings were to be, before he endured them. This
was given in his agony.[64]

That love—whose obedience is wide and long and high and
deep enough to dissolve a mountain of rightful wrath—is the
love you've been looking for all your life. No family love, no
friend love, no mother love, no spousal love, no romantic love—
nothing could possibly satisfy you like that. All those other kinds
of loves will let you down; this one never will.

SIXTEEN

THE SWORD

C John Sommerville, professor emeritus of history, currently at the University of Florida, carried out an exercise over several years with his students. He challenged his students to the following thought experiment: Imagine you see a little old lady coming down the street at night, and she's carrying a great big purse. It suddenly occurs to you that she's very little and very old, and it would be incredibly easy just to knock her over and grab the purse. But you don't. Why not? There are two possible answers. The answer of the shame-and-honor culture is that you don't do it because it would make you a despicable person, unworthy of respect. It would dishonor your family or your tribe. People would despise you for picking on the weak. You would despise yourself for picking on the weak. It wouldn't be strong—and it's critical that strength is respected. That approach, Professor Sommerville would point out, is self-regarding. You are thinking almost entirely of yourself and your tribe—about honor and reputation.

There's a second train of thought that would keep you from taking the purse. In the second train of thought, you would imagine how painful it would be to be mugged and how hard it would be for the woman if she depended on the money in her purse and it were taken from her. You ask yourself, "If I mug her, what will happen to her, and what will happen to the people who depend on her?" All else being equal, you want her to have a good life, so you don't do it. That's an other-regarding ethic— utterly different from the moral reasoning of a shame-and-honor culture. Having walked through these scenarios, Sommerville would ask his class, "All right, how many of you would take the purse?" Of course nobody would take it. Then he asked, "But why not? Which train of thought is yours?" And virtually everybody claimed the second train of thought.

Then he would make this observation to them: You may not realize it, but the idea that you put the other person ahead of yourself rather than thinking of yourself first, comes from Christianity. Your morals have been shaped by Christianity. Sommerville continued:

> An ethical system based on honor is a self-regarding ethic, while one based in charity is an other-regarding ethic. . . . With honor goes a concentration on pride rather than humility, dominance rather than service, courage rather than peaceableness, glory rather than modesty, loyalty rather than respect for all, generosity to one's friends rather than equality.

Sommerville goes on to say that the ethical system based on shame and honor was the system that dominated many civilizations before Christianity arrived. He then adds, "Students only have to

[184]

see this comparison on the blackboard to realize how Christian their moral orientation still is." Even though his students are very critical of the church and Christianity, "to give up Christian standards would leave [them] with no basis for [their] criticism." In effect, his students, in all their rants against Christianity, are "really asking for more of it, or a purer strain."[65]

What are these distinctly Christian ideas that still have such power to shape our own consciences and imaginations today?

All through the book of Mark—and all through Matthew, Luke, and John, too—Jesus is constantly talking about "the kingdom of heaven," "the kingdom of God," and also about "the kingdom of this world." A kingdom is an administration—that is, a way of ordering things and getting things done. For example, when a new coach comes to a team, there's a new administration. Or a new boss joins your department—that's a new administration. A new administration means things are different now; there's a new order for getting things done, a new set of assumptions and goals. What often distinguishes one administration from another is its list of values. The list is headed up with the things that really count; and in the middle would come things that are not so important. At the bottom, you would find things that are disdained or avoided. That's what makes the difference in how things are done. With a new administration, you begin to reorder your values, your goals. The old order of things is abolished a new order of things is instituted, and the way it's done is according to the list, whether or not the list is even written down.

If administrations and kingdoms are basically a matter of a list—which things are on the top, which things are on the bottom—then to order the list is, at some level, to order reality.

Of all the texts in which Jesus contrasts the kingdom of this world with the kingdom of God, the most succinct is in Luke 6. There, Jesus gives us two lists:

> *Blessed are you who are poor, for yours is the kingdom of God.*
> *Blessed are you who hunger now, for you will be satisfied.*
> *Blessed are you who weep now, for you will laugh.*
> *Blessed are you when men hate you, when they exclude you and insult you. . . .*
>
> (Luke 6:20–22)

> *But woe to you who are rich, for you have already received your comfort.*
> *Woe to you who are well fed now, for you will go hungry.*
> *Woe to you who laugh now, for you will mourn and weep.*
> *Woe to you when all men speak well of you.*
>
> (Luke 6:24–26)

Biblical scholar Michael Wilcock, in his study of this text, observes that in the life of God's people there will be a remarkable reversal of values: "Christians will prize what the world calls pitiable and suspect what the world calls desirable."[66] The things the world puts at the bottom of its list are at the top of the kingdom of God's list. And the things that are suspect in the kingdom of God are prized by the kingdom of this world. What's at the top of the list of the kingdom of this world? Power and money ("you who are rich"); success and recognition ("when all men speak well of you"). But what's at the top of God's list? Weakness and poverty ("you who are poor"); suffering and rejection ("when men hate you"). The list is inverted in the kingdom of God.

The First True Revolution

These two kingdoms, these two administrations of reality, these two sets of priorities and values meet dramatically in the Garden of Gethsemane:

> *Just as Jesus was speaking, Judas, one of the Twelve, appeared. With him was a crowd armed with swords and clubs, sent from the chief priests, the teachers of the law, and the elders. Now the betrayer had arranged a signal with them: "The one I kiss is the man; arrest him and lead him away under guard." Going at once to Jesus, Judas said, "Rabbi!" and kissed him. The men seized Jesus and arrested him.*
>
> (Mark 14:43–46)

The term *kiss of death* came into our English vocabulary from this incident. If you look it up in a dictionary, you'll see that the phrase means an intimacy with something that subsequently causes your destruction.

The problem is not that Judas is intimate with Jesus. Intimacy with Jesus is always the kiss of life, never the kiss of death. Judas's problem is that he's intimate with swords and clubs.

Why doesn't Judas just walk up to Jesus and say, "There he is, arrest him"? What's the kiss for? Why all the subterfuge? Was he expecting that Jesus would be armed with swords and clubs too? After all, Jesus talked about the kingdom of God, and any new kingdom had always used money, politics, military might, or some combination of these to get into power.

How does the King react to this kiss and to his arrest? Mark records:

The men seized Jesus and arrested him. Then one of those standing near drew his sword and struck the servant of the high priest, cutting off his ear. "Am I leading a rebellion," said Jesus, "that you have come out with swords and clubs to capture me? Every day I was with you, teaching in the temple courts, and you did not arrest me. But the Scriptures must be fulfilled."

(Mark 14:46–49)

Judas seems to be expecting armed resistance, otherwise he and his squad wouldn't be coming in this fashion. Jesus responds, "Am I leading a rebellion that you'd have to come with firepower and deception to capture me?" The word translated *rebellion* means a guerrilla movement that is using violent tactics (the sword) to overthrow the existing order of things and bring in a new order—a revolution. Jesus is saying, "If you come at me with swords, because you think I will retaliate with the sword, it shows you don't understand me at all. The kingdom of God is different from the kingdom of this world."

What Judas and those with him do not understand is that Jesus is indeed leading a revolution, but it is a different kind of revolution, and a much greater one than history has ever seen. What happens in the kingdom of this world is that revolutions basically keep the same old thing on top of the list. They're not real revolutions; money and power and politics always stay at the top. Most revolutions have been merely a fine-tuning of the same old order. Every revolution brings a new set of people into power, and then the next one puts a different set of people in power. But Jesus isn't just putting a new set of people in power; he is bringing a totally different administration of reality—the kingdom of God. Jesus is not a revolutionary you can stop with swords, because he's not about the sword at all. Judas doesn't get it.

[*188*]

But Judas is not the only one who doesn't get it. We read that when Jesus is arrested "one of those standing near drew his sword and struck the servant of the high priest, cutting off his ear." In the Gospel of John we're told it was Peter—which figures. Peter knows about the kingdom of God. He has heard Jesus's teaching about it over a period of years. Yet when push comes to shove, what's his instinct? Pull out that sword.

Aren't we kind of like Peter? We say we're on the side of justice, of peace, of fairness; but when a challenge arises, we feel for the sword hilt. We merge the kingdom of this world—sword on top, then money, power, success, and recognition—into our philosophy, whether it's Christianity or something else. We settle for the kiss of death. We're exactly like Peter.

To Peter and to all of us, Jesus is saying, "My kingdom is not of this world. It's completely different. This is how I'm going to change things: I'm going to put others ahead of myself. I'm going to love my enemies. I'm going to serve and sacrifice for others. I'm not going to repay evil with evil; I'm going to overcome evil with good. I will give up my power, my life. Weakness, poverty, suffering, and rejection will now be at the top of the list. My revolution comes without the sword; it is the first true revolution."

The Inversion of the Revolution

What do you think the disciples did as Jesus was arrested and was being led away by this armed and dangerous mob? Mark writes:

> *"Am I leading a rebellion," said Jesus, "that you have come out with swords and clubs to capture me? Every day I was with you, teaching in the temple courts, and you did not arrest me. But the Scriptures must be fulfilled."*

Then everyone deserted him and fled. A young man, wearing nothing but a linen garment, was following Jesus. When they seized him, he fled naked, leaving his garment behind.

(Mark 14:48–52)

"Then everyone deserted him and fled." Peter and the other disciples, who had spent years by his side, desert him at the first real test of their fortitude. One young man is so intent on saving his skin that when Judas's crowd grabs hold of his garment, he is willing to shed it and run away naked down the street. In the Bible, nakedness is a sign of shame and disgrace, and it's perfectly appropriate in this case: This man's an absolute coward, so the shame of running home naked suits the occasion. Some scholars say this is the author Mark himself, who would have been a young man at the time; if so, he's saying, "I was there and I was as bad as everybody else." Everyone has failed Jesus.

By recounting this young man's naked flight from the garden, Mark may be reminding us of another garden. In the Garden of Eden, too, there were people who were given a test, and they failed. They were exposed as naked and fled in shame. Centuries later, another garden and another test, and everybody fails in one way or another. They're either waving swords around or fleeing in naked shame.

But wait a minute—something is different. In the middle of *this* garden there's someone who is passing a test. Why are all the other people fleeing and failing? Their only reality is the world's sword. They're afraid somebody is going to arrest them, kill them, or start a revolution that will remove them from power. But Jesus is standing firm, and he's facing something even worse than the world's sword. Remember that when Adam and Eve were expelled from the garden, they turned around and saw the flaming sword of justice, keeping them from ever going back. Their sins separated them from God. There's no way back into the presence of God unless someone goes under the sword of divine justice. Jesus was in the garden facing the ultimate sword of divine justice, and he stood firm, for Adam and Eve, for me, for you.

Do you know why some people call the kingdom of this world "the right-side-up kingdom" and the kingdom of God "the upside-down kingdom?" The world's emphasis on power and recognition seems right-side up and natural, while Jesus's approach of service and sacrifice seems totally impossible and unnatural. For example, it's unnatural biologically—who ever heard of the survival of the weakest?

The kingdom of God also seems unnatural psychologically. When you hear Jesus say that he prizes weakness, poverty, suffering, and rejection, you say, "That's masochism. It's psychologically unhealthy. It's impossible to live like that."

And guess what, it *is* kind of impossible to live like that.

When you see Jesus caring for the poor, forgiving his enemies without bitterness, sacrificing his life for others, living a perfectly loving and perfectly sinless life, you say, "I can't do that." You're right—you can't. Jesus Christ as only an example will crush you; you will never be able to live up to it. But Jesus Christ as the Lamb will save you.

On the cross, Jesus is getting what we deserve so we can get what he deserves. When you see that this great reversal is for you, when you see that he gave up all his cosmic wealth and came into our poverty so that you could be spiritually rich, it changes you.

Say there's a person living completely in the values of the kingdom of this world and another person who is learning to belong to the kingdom of God, and each of them has a great job. Both suddenly learn they're about to lose their jobs, and they know they'll likely never recover that socioeconomic status. In the kingdom of this world, this feels like the end of your life. The kingdom of this world teaches you to base your identity on status, money, and power. Without them your identity is gutted. If you play by the rules of the kingdom of this world, you might do anything to keep your job. Maybe even lie or cheat or stab others in the back. But if you're starting to get rooted in the kingdom of God, you know losing your job is not going to be easy or pleasant, but you have learned that when weakness and suffering, poverty and rejection are near, the kingdom of God is near. It's the time when you come to grips with your real treasure, your real identity.

Christians are free to take or leave money, power, recognition, and status. How? These things at the top of the kingdom of this world don't have to control them the same way anymore. When you understand what Jesus has done for you, it frees you. When you realize that you are made righteous by his grace and not by your achievement, and that you are loved in Jesus Christ, it changes the way you look at power, money, and status; they don't control you anymore.

If you're trying to save yourself, trying to earn your own self-esteem, trying to prove yourself, you'll either hate money and power too much or love them too much. For example, you may say you don't like money and power and don't like people who have them. Staying away from them makes you feel noble. In that case you're basically a self-saver. Or perhaps instead you desperately *need* money and status, for the same reason: You're a self-saver. You may despise other kinds of self-salvation more than yours, but you're basically doing the same thing in a different way. But if you know you're a sinner saved by sheer grace, you can take it or leave it. You're free. If money or power comes, there's a lot you can do with it. But if it starts to go, you know that's one of the ways the power of God's Kingdom is going to work in your life. The sword is exiting from your life. The compulsion is dissipating. You work but your work does not define you. You work but it's not driving you into the ground. And you're going to be so content, you'll almost look reckless. People will say, "How can you spend your money like that? How can you let that career opportunity go by? How can you be involved with such a needy person when you know she will probably take advantage of you?" A Christian can respond, "It's not the end of the world if somebody takes advantage of me, or if my money is gone, or if my career doesn't develop as I might like. I'm not controlled by that fear anymore." You are replacing the kingdom of this world with the kingdom of God.

In Daniel 5, Belshazzar, king of Babylon, is having a wild party, an orgy, and doesn't know that an army is on the march to sack the city and kill him that very night. But in the midst of the party, a hand appears and starts writing on the wall. The message says, "Your days are numbered."

If you're living for yourself, spending all your money on yourself, striving for power, focusing on your success and your reputation, you may be having a wonderful party, but according to the Bible, that kingdom is going to be inverted. The days of that kingdom are numbered.

SEVENTEEN

THE END

They took Jesus to the high priest, and all the chief priests, elders, and teachers of the law came together. Peter followed him at a distance, right into the courtyard of the high priest. There he sat with the guards and warmed himself at the fire. The chief priests and the whole Sanhedrin were looking for evidence against Jesus so that they could put him to death, but they did not find any. Many testified falsely against him, but their statements did not agree. Then some stood up and gave this false testimony against him: "We heard him say, 'I will destroy this man-made temple and in three days will build another, not made by man.'" Yet even then their testimony did not agree.

(Mark 14:53–59)

There's nothing more dramatic than to be on trial for your life, and no more dramatic moment in a trial than when the defendant is called to testify on the witness stand. And perhaps there's never been a more dramatic and shocking testimony given on a witness stand than the one Jesus Christ gave during his trial. Mark continues:

> *Then the high priest stood up before them and asked Jesus, "Are you not going to answer? What is this testimony that these men are bringing against you?" But Jesus remained silent and gave no answer. Again the high priest asked him, "Are you the Christ, the Son of the Blessed One?" "I am," said Jesus. "And you will see the Son of Man sitting at the right hand of the Mighty One and coming on the clouds of heaven."*
>
> (Mark 14:60–62)

The high priest puts Jesus on the witness stand, as it were, and asks if he is the Christ (the "Messiah"), the Son of the Blessed One. At other times in the Gospel of Mark, Jesus has avoided similar lines of inquiry about his identity (Mark 7:5–6) or turned the question back on the questioner (Mark 11:29). This time, Jesus answers this central question of the Gospel of Mark head on—positively and fully. "I am," said Jesus. "And you will see the Son of Man sitting at the right hand of the Mighty One and coming on the clouds of heaven."

By saying "*I am*," Jesus claims to be the Messiah, the promised one. However, we should remember that, in general, the Jews did not expect the Christ to be literally divine. Therefore, Jesus goes on to amplify the meaning of the label *Messiah* by identifying himself as the *Son of Man* and also by saying he will sit at the right hand of God.

In both of Jesus's biblical allusions here ("Son of Man" from Daniel 7:13, and "at his right hand" from Psalm 110:1), the Messiah comes as a judge. Everybody in the room—all of the ruling council of the Sanhedrin—knows who the Son of Man is. In Daniel 7, the Son of Man comes from the throne of God to earth in the clouds of heaven to judge the world. And the clouds of heaven are not the same as the clouds of earth, just water vapor. These clouds are the *shekinah* glory, the very presence of God. Therefore by replying as he does, Jesus is saying: "I will come to earth in the very glory of God and judge the entire world." It's an astounding statement. It's a claim to deity.

Of all the things Jesus could have said—and there are so many texts, themes, images, metaphors, and passages of the Hebrew Scriptures that he could have used to tell who he was—he specifically says he's the judge. By his choice of text, Jesus is deliberately forcing us to see the paradox. There's been an enormous reversal. He is the judge over the entire world, being judged by the world. He should be in the judgment seat, and we should be in the dock, in chains. Everything is turned upside down.

And as soon as Jesus claims to be this judge, as soon as he claims deity, the response is explosive. Mark writes:

> *"I am," said Jesus. "And you will see the Son of Man sitting at the right hand of the Mighty One and coming on the clouds of heaven." The high priest tore his clothes. "Why do we need any more witnesses?" he asked. "You have heard the blasphemy. What do you think?" They all condemned him as worthy of death. Then some began to spit at him; they blindfolded him, struck him with their fists, and said, "Prophesy!" And the guards took him and beat him.*
>
> (Mark 14:62–65)

The high priest rips his own garments apart, a sign of the greatest possible outrage, horror, and grief. And then the whole trial deteriorates. In fact it's no longer a trial; it's a riot. The jurors and judges begin to spit on him and beat him. In the middle of the trial, they go absolutely berserk. He is instantly convicted of blasphemy and condemned as worthy of death.

But the court of the Sanhedrin did not have the power to pass this death sentence. It was empowered to judge many cases, but capital cases needed the confirmation of the Roman procurator. As soon as they are able, the Sanhedrin hands Jesus over to Pilate, the governor appointed by Rome, so that he can put Jesus to death. Mark continues:

> *Very early in the morning, the chief priests, with the elders, the teachers of the law, and the whole Sanhedrin, reached a decision. They bound Jesus, led him away and handed him over to Pilate. "Are you the king of the Jews?" asked Pilate. "Yes, it is as you say," Jesus replied. The chief priests accused him of many things. So again Pilate asked him, "Aren't you going to answer? See how many things they are accusing you of." But Jesus still made no reply, and Pilate was amazed.*
>
> (Mark 15:1–5)

Jesus is on trial again, this time before Pilate. The religious leaders offer a battery of charges. Jesus does not answer them, to the marvel of Pilate. We know from the other Gospel writers that Pilate has no desire at all to try this case. He vacillates and stalls in an attempt to get out of it. But he has another card to play: He may be able to escape the responsibility of a decision through the time-honored custom of releasing a prisoner amid a time of general rejoicing:

> *Now it was the custom at the Feast to release a prisoner whom the people requested. A man called Barabbas was*

in prison with the insurrectionists who had committed murder in the uprising. The crowd came up and asked Pilate to do for them what he usually did. "Do you want me to release to you the king of the Jews?" asked Pilate, knowing it was out of envy that the chief priests had handed Jesus over to him.

(Mark 15:6–10)

Pilate is still trying to find a way out. He knows that the religious leaders are only accusing Jesus out of envy; they don't have a case. Barabbas is a violent man who has been convicted of murder. Will Pilate knowingly free a guilty man and condemn an innocent one? Mark continues:

But the chief priests stirred up the crowd to have Pilate release Barabbas instead. "What shall I do, then, with the one you call the king of the Jews?" Pilate asked them. "Crucify him!" they shouted. "Why? What crime has he committed?" asked Pilate. But they shouted all the louder, "Crucify him!" Wanting to satisfy the crowd, Pilate released Barabbas to them. He had Jesus flogged, and handed him over to be crucified.

(Mark 15:11–15)

Pilate is extremely reluctant to execute Jesus, but despite pronouncing that Jesus is not guilty of a capital offense, he hands him over to be crucified.

Crucifixion was designed to be the most humiliating and gruesome method of execution. The Romans reserved it for their worst offenders. It was a protracted, bloody, public spectacle of extreme pain that usually ended in a horrible death by shock or asphyxiation. But it is noteworthy that Mark gives us very few of the gory details.

He aims his spotlight away from the physical horrors of Jesus's ordeal in order to focus it on the deeper meaning behind the events. He simply records:

> *Then they led him out to crucify him. A certain man from Cyrene, Simon, the father of Alexander and Rufus, was passing by on his way in from the country, and they forced him to carry the cross. They brought Jesus to the place called Golgotha (which means The Place of the Skull). Then they offered him wine mixed with myrrh, but he did not take it. And they crucified him. Dividing up his clothes, they cast lots to see what each would get.*
>
> (Mark 15:20–24)

Although Mark makes no explicit reference to the fulfillment of prophecy, his choice of wording here shows that he is thinking of Psalm 22:

> *All who see me mock me; they hurl insults, shaking their heads. . . . I am poured out like water, and all my bones are out of joint. My heart has turned to wax; it has melted away within me. . . . Dogs have surrounded me; a band of evil men has encircled me, they have pierced my hands and my feet. I can count all my bones; people stare and gloat over me. They divide my garments among them and cast lots for my clothing.*
>
> (Psalm 22:7, 14, 16–18)

Imagine what Jesus's followers felt as they watched this scene around the cross, as they watched the man they had followed for years being crucified. Here was a man who calmed storms, banished sickness, and cheated death by the miraculous power of his word. Here was a man who less than a week before had been given a king's welcome to Jerusalem. Here was the Christ. How could this be happening? Mark goes on:

> *It was the third hour when they crucified him. The writ-ten notice of the charge against him read: THE KING OF THE JEWS. They crucified two robbers with him, one on his right and one on his left. Those who passed by hurled insults at him, shaking their heads and saying, "So! You who are going to destroy the temple and build it in three days, come down from the cross and save your-self!" In the same way the chief priests and the teachers of the law mocked him among themselves. "He saved oth-ers," they said, "but he can't save himself! Let this Christ, this King of Israel, come down now from the cross, that we may see and believe." Those crucified with him also heaped insults on him. At the sixth hour darkness came over the whole land until the ninth hour.*
>
> (Mark 15:25–33)

In their depictions of Jesus's death, Mark and the other three Gospel writers show a consistent concern for what visual artists call "values"—that is, the interplay and contrast between dark-ness and light. All four Gospel writers take pains to show us that all the critical events of Jesus's death happened *in the dark*. The betrayal and the trial before the Sanhedrin all happened at night, of course, but now at the actual moment of Jesus's death, though it is daytime, an inexplicable darkness descends. "At the sixth hour darkness came over the whole land until the ninth hour." The sixth hour was noon; the ninth hour was 3:00 p.m. So from 12:00 to 3:00 in the afternoon, as Jesus was dying, there was total darkness.

Many people have proposed a natural cause for this event—an eclipse, for instance. But a solar eclipse does not create absolute darkness for more than a few minutes. Further, a solar eclipse can't happen during the time of a full moon, and Passover is always celebrated at a full moon. Other people have suggested that the cause was a desert windstorm of the type that can kick up enough dust to obscure the sun for days at a time. But Passover falls in the wet season, so this darkness couldn't have come from a windstorm.

This was a supernatural darkness.

In the Bible, darkness during the day is a recognized sign of God's displeasure and judgment.[67] The supreme example of that phenomenon is the darkness over Egypt that was the penultimate plague at the time of the first Passover (Exodus 10:21–23). So when this darkness fell, we know that God was acting in judgment. But who was God judging? Mark continues:

> *At the sixth hour darkness came over the whole land until the ninth hour. And at the ninth hour Jesus cried out in a loud voice, "Eloi, Eloi, lama sabachthani?"—which means, "My God, my God, why have you forsaken me?"*
>
> (Mark 15:33–34)

When Jesus started to cry out, he didn't say, "My friends, my friends!" "My head, my head!" "My hands, my hands!" He said, "My God, my God." On the cross, Jesus was forsaken by God.

He said, "*My* God." That's the language of intimacy. To call anyone "my Susan" or "my John" is affectionate. And biblically, "my God" is covenantal address. It was the way God said someone could address him if he or she had a personal relationship with him. *"You shall be my people, and I shall be your God."*

"My God, you have forsaken me." If after a service some

Sunday morning one of the members of my church comes to me and says, "I never want to see you or talk to you again," I will feel pretty bad. But if today my wife comes up to me and says, "I never want to see you or talk to you again," that's a lot worse. The longer the love, the deeper the love, the greater the torment of its loss.

But this forsakenness, this loss, was between the Father and the Son, who had loved each other from all eternity. This love was infinitely long, absolutely perfect, and Jesus was losing it. Jesus was being cut out of the dance.

Jesus, the Maker of the world, was being unmade. Why? Jesus was experiencing our judgment day. "My God, my God, why have you forsaken me?" It wasn't a rhetorical question. And the answer is: For you, for me, for us. Jesus was forsaken by God so that we would never have to be. The judgment that should have fallen on us fell instead on Jesus.

Darkness and Disintegration

These days most of us don't know what real physical darkness is. Even when we are out in the country at night, there are always towns nearby with plenty of electric lights. If you're in *utter* darkness, though, you can't even see your hand in front of your face. And to stay in utter darkness for an extended time can have a radically disorienting effect on you. In 1914, British explorer Ernest Shackleton and his crew took a ship to Antarctica. Their plan was to land, walk across Antarctica, cross over the South Pole, and continue all the way across. The plan had to be abandoned, though, because their ship, the *Endurance*, got caught in polar ice and was crushed. Over the following months, Shackleton's crew fought just to survive and to get home. One of Shackleton's biographers says that of all the difficulties they faced—including starvation and frigid temperatures—the worst thing was the darkness. Near the South Pole, the sun goes down in mid-May and doesn't come back up until late July. There's no daytime—no sunlight—for more than two months.

In all the world, say the biographers of polar explorers, there is no desolation more complete than the polar night. Only those who have experienced it can fully appreciate what it means to be without the sun day after day and week after week. Few unaccustomed to it can fight off its effects altogether, and it has driven some men mad. In such deep darkness you can't see forward, so you don't know where you're going. You have no direction. You can't even see yourself; you don't know what you look like. You may as well have no identity. And you can't tell whether there is anyone around you, friend or foe. You are isolated. Physical darkness brings disorientation, but according to the Bible, so does spiritual darkness. Spiritual darkness comes when we turn away from God as our true light and make something else the center of our life.

The Bible sometimes compares God to the sun.[68] The sun is a source of visual truth, because by it we see everything. And the sun is a source of biological life, because without it nothing could live. And God, the Bible says, is *the* source of *all* truth and *all* life. If you orbit around God, then your life has truth and vitality. You are in the light. But if you turn away from God and orbit around anything else—your career, a relationship, your family—as the source of your warmth and your hope, the result is spiritual darkness. You are turning away from the truth, away from life, toward darkness.

When you are in spiritual darkness, although you may feel your life is headed in the right direction, you are actually profoundly disoriented.

If anything but God is more important to you, you have a problem with direction. It's impossible to discern where you're going, let alone where you *ought* to be going. Money, career, love—for a period of time you may feel you have something to live for. But if you actually get the thing you have been seeking, you suddenly realize that it's not big enough for your soul. It doesn't produce its own light.

Also, if you center on anything but God, you suffer a loss of identity. Your identity will be fragile and insecure, because it's based on the things you center your life on. It's based on human approval. It's based on how well you perform. You don't really know who you are. In the darkness you can't see yourself.

Moreover, in spiritual darkness you are isolated. You are wrapped up in the things that you're living for, so you're always scared or angry or proud or driven or full of self-pity. As a result, you become isolated from other people.

Let me illustrate this personally. I want to be a good minister and a good preacher. But if achieving those goals becomes my real source of hope, my significance, my security, more important to me than God's love for me in Jesus, I experience a loss of identity. A pastor is always subject to criticism, and as I wrote in chapter 11, that can be discouraging when it inevitably happens. But if my preaching and ministry are my ultimate center and I get criticism, then I'm overcome with insecurity. Or when I fail to perform up to my expectations, I'm devastated. Inordinate guilt churns inside me. In the end I begin to disintegrate. Similarly, if two people love each other more than they love God, then minor fights will become major fights, and major fights will become world-shaking cataclysms, because neither can take the other's displeasure or the other's failure. They become isolated from each other and eventually their relationship begins to disintegrate.

Spiritual darkness—turning away from God, the true light,

and making anything more important than him—leads invariably from disorientation to disintegration. And, apart from the intervention of God, we are all in spiritual darkness. We are all orbiting around something else. And we're all incapable of changing our orbit, because we inevitably, ultimately, seek to glorify ourselves instead of God. So we are all on a trajectory toward a life of disintegration.

But that trajectory won't stop at the end of our lives. When God returns he will judge every action, every thought, every longing—everything our heart has ever produced. And if there is anything imperfect, then we will not be able to remain in his presence. And being out of the presence of God, who is all light and all truth, means utter darkness and eternal disintegration. The biblical prophets describe this final day of judgment:

> *See, the day of the LORD is coming—a cruel day, with wrath and fierce anger—to make the land desolate and destroy the sinners within it. The stars of heaven and their constellations will not show their light. The rising sun will be darkened and the moon will not give its light. . . . I will put an end to the arrogance of the haughty and will humble the pride of the ruthless. . . . I will make the heavens tremble; and the earth will shake from its place at the wrath of the LORD Almighty, in the day of his burning anger.*
>
> (Isaiah 13:9–13)

> *The LORD has sworn by the Pride of Jacob: "I will never forget anything they have done." Will not the land tremble for this, and all who live in it mourn? The whole land will rise like the Nile; it will be stirred up and then sink like*

the river of Egypt. "In that day," declares the Sovereign
LORD, "I will make the sun go down at noon and darken
the earth in broad daylight. I will turn your religious
feasts into mourning and all your singing into weeping."

(Amos 8:7–10)

This was our trajectory, and Jesus's death was the only way to alter it. This is why Jesus had to go to the cross. He fell into the complete darkness for which we were headed. He died the death we should have died, so that we can be saved from this judgment and instead live in the light and presence of God. And how do we know it worked? Back to Mark:

When some of those standing near heard this, they said,
"Listen, he's calling Elijah." One man ran, filled a sponge
with wine vinegar, put it on a stick, and offered it to Jesus
to drink. "Now leave him alone. Let's see if Elijah comes to
take him down," he said. With a loud cry, Jesus breathed
his last. The curtain of the temple was torn in two from
top to bottom. And when the centurion, who stood there in
front of Jesus, heard his cry and saw how he died, he said,
"Surely this man was the Son of God!"

(Mark 15:35–39)

Remember that the curtain in the temple was not a flimsy little veil; it was heavy and thick, almost as substantial as a wall. The curtain separated the holy of holies, where God's *shekinah* glory dwelled, from the rest of the temple—it separated the people from the presence of God. And remember that only the holiest man, the high priest, from the holiest nation, the Jews, could enter the holy of holies—and only on the holiest day of the year, Yom Kippur, and he had to bring a blood sacrifice, an atonement for sins. The curtain said loudly and clearly that it is impossible for anyone sinful—anyone in spiritual darkness—to come into God's presence.

At the moment Jesus Christ died, this massive curtain was ripped open. The tear was from top to bottom, just to make clear who did it. This was God's way of saying, "This is the sacrifice that ends all sacrifices, the way is now open to approach me." Now that Jesus has died, anybody who believes in him can see God, connect to God. The barrier is gone for good. Our trajectory has been permanently redirected toward God. And that's only possible because Jesus has just paid the price for our sin. Anybody who believes can go in now.

To make sure we get the point, Mark immediately shows us the first person who went in: the centurion. His confession, "Surely this man was the Son of God," is momentous. Why? Because the first line in the first chapter of Mark refers to "Jesus Christ, the Son of God." Up to this point in Mark, no human being had figured that out. The disciples had called him the Christ, though in the prevailing culture the Christ was not considered to be divine. All along, Jesus's teachings and acts of power—and even his testimony in front of the chief priests—had been pointing to the fact that he was divine. And people had been asking, "Who is this?" But the first person to get it was the centurion who presided over his death.

This was even more unlikely because he was Roman. Every Roman coin of the time was inscribed "Tiberius Caesar, son of the divine Augustus." The only person a loyal Roman would ever call "Son of God" was Caesar—but this man gave the title to Jesus. And he was a hard character. Centurions were not aristocrats who got military commissions; they were enlisted men who had risen through the ranks. So this man had seen death, and had inflicted it, to a degree that you and I can hardly imagine.

Here was a hardened, brutal man. Yet something had penetrated his spiritual darkness. He became the first person to confess the deity of Jesus Christ.

There is a striking contrast between the centurion and everyone else around the cross. The disciples—who had been taught by Jesus repeatedly and at length that this day would come—were completely confused and stymied. The religious leaders had looked at the very deepest wisdom of God and rejected it.

What penetrated the centurion's darkness? How did he suddenly come into the light? For some thirty years I have been thinking about this question, trying to figure out why it was the centurion who first understood who Jesus was. Here's what I believe shone the light into his darkness: The centurion heard Jesus's cry, and saw how Jesus died.

I have only ever seen one person actually breathe his last breath. I'll never forget that experience. Very likely you, too, have been present for a death only once or twice, if at all. But the centurion had seen many people die—and many of those by his own hand. Yet even for him this death was unique. He saw something about Jesus's death that was unlike any other. The tenderness of Jesus, despite the terror, must have pierced right through his hardness. The beauty of Jesus in his death must have flooded his darkness with light.

The Beauty of the Darkness

Christianity is the only religious faith that says that God himself actually suffered, actually cried out in suffering. Now what good is that? To Jesus's followers assembled around the cross, it certainly seemed senseless: that there was no good in it at all. But in fact they came to realize that Jesus's suffering was of immense good to them, as can we. Why? Because they would eventually see that they had been looking right at the greatest act of God's love, power, and justice in history. God came into the world and suffered and died on the cross in order to save us. It is the ultimate proof of his love for us.

And when *you* suffer, you may be completely in the dark about the reason for your own suffering. It may seem as senseless to you as Jesus's suffering seemed to the disciples. But the cross tells you what the reason *isn't*. It can't be that God doesn't love you; it can't be that he has no plan for you. It can't be that he has abandoned you. Jesus was abandoned, and paid for our sins, so that God the Father would never abandon you. The cross proves that he loves you and understands what it means to suffer. It also demonstrates that God can be working in your life even when it seems like there is no rhyme or reason to what is happening.

Even Albert Camus, the famous existentialist, realized that if you look at the cross, you could no longer go through suffering in the same way. Camus said this:

> The God-man also suffers, and does so with patience. . . .
> he too is shattered and dies. The night on Golgotha only
> has so much significance for man because in its darkness
> the Godhead, visibly renouncing all inherited privileges,
> endures to the end the anguish of death, including the
> depths of despair.[69]

Jesus Christ not only died the death we should have died—he also lived the life we should have lived but can't. His was perfect obedience, in our place. It doesn't matter who you are—centurion, prostitute, hit man, minister. The curtain has been ripped from top to bottom. The barrier is gone. There is forgiveness and grace for you.

By saying the centurion "heard his cry," Mark is pressing the story right up to your ear. If you listen closely to that cry—*My*

God, my God, why have you forsaken me?—you can see the same beauty, the same tenderness. If you see Jesus losing the infinite love of his Father out of his infinite love for you, it will melt your hardness. No matter who you are, it will open your eyes and shatter your darkness. You will at long last be able to turn away from all those other things that are dominating your life, addicting you, drawing you away from God. Jesus Christ's darkness can dispel and destroy our own, so that in the place of hardness and darkness and death we have tenderness and light and life.

The only time I ever faced death personally was when I had thyroid cancer. From the beginning the doctors told me it was treatable. Still, when I was going under anesthesia for the surgery, I wondered what would happen. You may be curious about what passage from the Bible came to my mind. True confession: What I thought of was a passage from *Lord of the Rings*. It comes near the end of the third book, when evil and darkness seem overwhelming. Here is what Tolkien tells us about the thoughts of Sam, one of the heroes:

> Sam saw a white star twinkle for a while. The beauty of it smote his heart, as he looked up out of the forsaken land, and hope returned to him. For like a shaft, clear and cold, the thought pierced him that in the end the Shadow was only a small and passing thing: there was light and high beauty forever beyond its reach. His song in the Tower had been defiance rather than hope; for then he was thinking of himself. Now, for a moment, his own fate . . . ceased to trouble him. . . . [P]utting away all fear, he cast himself into a deep, untroubled sleep.[70]

I remember thinking at that moment: It's really true. Because of Jesus's death evil is a passing thing—a shadow. There is light and high beauty forever beyond its reach because evil fell into the heart of Jesus. The only darkness that could have destroyed us forever fell into his heart. It didn't matter what happened in my surgery—it was going to be all right. And it *is* going to be all right.

EIGHTEEN

THE BEGINNING

In the decades before and after Jesus's life and death there were dozens of messianic movements in Israel. In almost every case the messianic leader was killed, in many cases by execution, and after the leader's death each of these movements invariably collapsed. Everybody went home, and that was it. Of all those dozens of movements, only one did not collapse after the death of the leader. Not only did it not collapse, it exploded: In the course of about three hundred years it had spread through the entire Roman empire.

Out of all those messianic movements, what made the Christian faith different? Christians would say it is because of what happened *after* the leader of this movement was killed. So what did happen to cause explosive growth in Christianity after its founder's death? Let's return to Mark:

> *With a loud cry, Jesus breathed his last. The curtain of the temple was torn in two from top to bottom. And when*

the centurion, who stood there in front of Jesus, heard his cry and saw how he died, he said, "Surely this man was the Son of God!" Some women were watching from a distance. Among them were Mary Magdalene, Mary the mother of James the younger and of Joses, and Salome. In Galilee these women had followed him and cared for his needs. Many other women who had come up with him to Jerusalem were also there. It was Preparation Day (that is, the day before the Sabbath). So as evening approached, Joseph of Arimathea, a prominent member of the Council, who was himself waiting for the kingdom of God, went boldly to Pilate and asked for Jesus' body.

(Mark 15:37–43)

Jesus died in mid-afternoon and the Sabbath began at sunset. The Jewish law permitted no work on the Sabbath, which meant they could not bury the body of Jesus that night or the next day. So Joseph goes to Pilate, hoping to be able to bury the body in time. Joseph, though a Pharisee, shows enormous courage and independence of thought by asking for Jesus's body. Mark reports:

Pilate was surprised to hear that he was already dead. Summoning the centurion, he asked him if Jesus had already died. When he learned from the centurion that it was so, he gave the body to Joseph. So Joseph bought some linen cloth, took down the body, wrapped it in the linen, and placed it in a tomb cut out of rock. Then he rolled a stone against the entrance of the tomb. Mary Magdalene and Mary the mother of Joses saw where he was laid.

(Mark 15:44–47)

The way Mark reports the burial is significant: He is "certifying" that Jesus was really dead. Joseph of Arimathea is named here as an identified witness who actually had Jesus's body wrapped up and sealed it in a tomb. A Roman centurion (who would be an expert) bore witness of Jesus's death to Pilate (who would be the legal authority on the matter). Finally, two women are cited as eyewitnesses to the burial. So multiple experts and witnesses prove he was really dead. But Mark has more to say:

> *When the Sabbath was over, Mary Magdalene, Mary the mother of James, and Salome bought spices so that they might go to anoint Jesus' body. Very early on the first day of the week, just after sunrise, they were on their way to the tomb and they asked each other, "Who will roll the stone away from the entrance of the tomb?"*
>
> (Mark 16:1–3)

There is a strange redundancy in Mark's account: Three times within a span of just eight lines, Mark records the names of some women who witnessed these events: Mary Magdalene, Mary the mother of James and Joses, and Salome. Biblical scholar Richard Bauckham says that this is another way Mark is letting us know that he is recording a historical account, not writing a legend. The repeated names of the women here are source citations—we could call them footnotes. These women must have been alive at the time that Mark was writing, or he wouldn't have cited their names repeatedly. By including their names, Mark was saying to anyone reading this document: "If you want to check out the truth of my story, go talk to these three women. They're still alive, and they can corroborate everything I have said."[71] So what is it that these women witness? They have brought spices and are on their way to the tomb to finish the burial rites on Jesus's dead body. Mark writes:

> . . . *they asked each other, "Who will roll the stone away from the entrance of the tomb?" But when they looked up, they saw that the stone, which was very large, had been rolled away. As they entered the tomb, they saw a young man dressed in a white robe sitting on the right side, and they were alarmed. "Don't be alarmed," he said. "You are looking for Jesus the Nazarene, who was crucified. He has risen! He is not here. See the place where they laid him. But go, tell his disciples and Peter, 'He is going ahead of you into Galilee. There you will see him, just as he told you.'"*
>
> (Mark 16:3–7)

"He has risen! He is not here." Can you imagine how these women felt, what they were thinking, as they heard these words? They had come to the tomb expecting to find a dead body. Instead they hear the words: "He has risen! He is not here."

But they shouldn't have been completely surprised. Recall that repeatedly in this Gospel, Jesus has said to his disciples, "I will rise on the third day." He said it in Mark 8, again in Mark 9, and yet again in Mark 10. As you've seen, Mark's writing is characterized by great economy of style; his accounts are short and to the point. If, then, Mark quotes Jesus saying something three times, it probably means that Jesus was saying this over and over again. *I will die, but I'll rise on the third day. I will rise on the third day. I will rise on the third day. I will rise on the third day.*

Given that repetition, something curious is going on. On the third day after Jesus's death, there are no male disciples around;

these female disciples do appear, but they are bringing along all the expensive spices and perfumes with which a *dead* body was customarily anointed. Nobody is expecting a resurrection. If you were the Gospel writer Mark, trying to write a credible piece of fiction, and you have had Jesus saying repeatedly to his disciples that he would rise on the third day, wouldn't you have at least one disciple thinking this through after Jesus's death and saying to the others, "Hey, it's the third day. Maybe we ought to go take a look at Jesus's tomb. What can it hurt?" That would only be reasonable. But nobody said anything like that. In fact, they did not expect a resurrection at all. It didn't occur to them. The angel in front of the empty tomb had to remind the women: "You will see him, *just as he told you*." If Mark had made up this story, he wouldn't have written it this way.

And here's the point: The resurrection was as inconceivable for the first disciples, as impossible for them to believe, as it is for many of us today. Granted, their reasons would have been different from ours. The Greeks did not believe in resurrection; in the Greek worldview, the afterlife was liberation of the soul from the body. For them resurrection would never be part of life after death. As for the Jews, some of them believed in a future general resurrection when the entire world would be renewed, but they had no concept of an individual rising from the dead. The people of Jesus's day were not predisposed to believe in resurrection any more than we are.

Celsus, a Greek philosopher who lived in the second century A.D., was highly antagonistic to Christianity and wrote a number of works listing arguments against it. One of the arguments he believed most telling went like this: Christianity can't be true, because the written accounts of the resurrection are based on the testimony of women—and we all know that women are hysterical. And many of Celsus's readers agreed: For them, that was a major problem. In ancient societies, as you know, women were marginalized, and the testimony of women was never given much credence.

Do you see what that means? If Mark and the Christians were making up these stories to get their movement off the ground, they would never have written women into the story as the first eyewitnesses to Jesus's empty tomb. The only possible reason for the presence of women in these accounts is that they really were present and reported what they saw. The stone has been rolled away, the tomb is empty, and an angel declares that Jesus is risen.

The angel then instructs the women, "Go, tell his disciples and Peter. He is going ahead of you into Galilee. There you will see him." Consider what he could have said: "You tell those faithless, backstabbing cowards that Jesus might deign to see them if they grovel—and they'd better grovel well." A message like that would have been perfectly warranted. We've seen what the disciples did to Jesus. But Jesus's message to the disciples here, through the angel, was "I will see you. I'm going ahead of you. I'll be waiting for you. I want you back." For details of that meeting we go to Luke's Gospel:

> While they [the disciples] were still talking about this, Jesus himself stood among them and said to them, "Peace be with you." They were startled and frightened, thinking they saw a ghost. He said to them, "Why are you troubled, and why do doubts rise in your minds? Look at my hands and my feet. It is I myself! Touch me and see; a ghost does not have flesh and bones, as you see I have." When he had said this, he showed them his hands and feet. . . . He said to them, "This is what I told you while I was still with

you. . . . This is what is written: The Christ will suffer
and rise from the dead on the third day. . . ."

(Luke 24:36–46)

What was the resurrected Jesus like? Well, Jesus's resurrection body had "flesh and bones." He was not a ghost. The disciples were able to recognize him and to touch him. He spoke with them. But could they all have been having a group hallucination?

No, because the disciples were not the only ones who saw and touched Jesus. Paul makes a long list of people who claimed to have seen the risen Christ personally, and notes that *"most of them are still living"* (1 Corinthians 15:6). How could Paul write that "Peter said he saw the risen Jesus" if Peter was saying, "No, I didn't"?

Paul mentions five appearances of the risen Christ, including five hundred people at one "sighting." Seven appearances are recounted in the four Gospels. And Acts 1:3–4 tells us that for forty days Jesus appeared constantly to numerous groups of people. The size of the groups and the number of the sightings make it virtually impossible to conclude that all these people had hallucinations. Either they must have actually seen Jesus, or hundreds of people must have been part of an elaborate conspiracy that lasted for decades. Paul suggests to his readers that they can go and talk to any of the five hundred witnesses they like. If this was a hoax, it would have had to last for years, and each of the dozens of conspirators would have had to take the secret to his grave.

Moreover, there has to be some explanation for how the cowardly group of disciples was transformed into a group of leaders. Many of them went on to live sacrificial lives, and many of them were killed for teaching that Jesus had been resurrected.

Three fundamental lines of evidence intertwine to convince

us that Jesus rose from the dead: the fact of the empty tomb, the testimony of numerous eyewitnesses, and the long-term impact on the lives of Jesus's followers.

Jesus had risen, just as he told them he would. After a criminal does his time in jail and fully satisfies the sentence, the law has no more claim on him and he walks out free. Jesus Christ came to pay the penalty for our sins. That was an infinite sentence, but he must have satisfied it fully, because on Easter Sunday he walked out free. The resurrection was God's way of stamping PAID IN FULL right across history so that nobody could miss it.

He Has Done It

When Jesus cried out from the cross, "My God, my God, why have you forsaken me?" he was echoing Psalm 22, which foretold the circumstances of the cross and what it would accomplish. This same psalm predicted that Jesus would be mocked and that they would cast lots for his clothing. Toward its end, Psalm 22 moves from suffering to deliverance:

> *Deliver my life from the sword, my precious life from the power of the dogs. Rescue me from the mouth of the lions; save me from the horns of the wild oxen. . . . For he has not despised or disdained the suffering of the afflicted one; he has not hidden his face from him but has listened to his cry for help. . . . All the ends of the earth will remember and turn to the LORD, and all the families of the nations will bow down before him, for dominion belongs to the LORD and he rules over the nations. All the rich of the earth will feast and worship; all who go down to the dust*

will kneel before him—those who cannot keep themselves alive. . . . They will proclaim his righteousness to a people yet unborn—for he has done it.

(Psalm 22:20–21, 24, 27–29, 31)

If Jesus really has done it—if he truly is risen—it means the story of the world according to Mark is all true. Jesus really is the Son of God, the true and perfect King; he came to earth to die on the cross for us; and by trusting in what he has done there, we are spared from eternal judgment and ushered into the presence of God for all eternity. In the Gospel of John, Jesus puts it this way:

"I am the resurrection and the life. He who believes in me will live, even though he dies; and whoever lives and believes in me will never die."

(John 11:25–26)

His death means no death for us. His resurrection means our resurrection.

We believe that Jesus died and rose again and so we believe that God will bring with Jesus those who have fallen asleep in him.

(1 Thessalonians 4:14)

But if Jesus is *not* risen, then the story of the world that Mark has been telling is just fiction. Paul makes this trenchantly clear:

If there is no resurrection of the dead, then not even Christ has been raised. And if Christ has not been raised, our preaching is useless and so is your faith. More than

that, we are then found to be false witnesses about God,
for we have testified about God that he raised Christ from
the dead. But he did not raise him if in fact the dead are
not raised. For if the dead are not raised, then Christ has
not been raised either. And if Christ has not been raised,
your faith is futile; you are still in your sins. Then those
also who have fallen asleep in Christ are lost. If only for
this life we have hope in Christ, we are to be pitied more
than all men.

(1 Corinthians 15:13–19)

The truth of the resurrection is of supreme and eternal importance. It is the hinge upon which the story of the world pivots.

A Remembrance of the Future

What if you believe the resurrection is true? You believe that
Jesus has died to save you—to redirect your eternal trajectory
irrevocably toward God. You believe that God has accepted you,
for Jesus's sake, through an act of supreme grace. You are part of
the kingdom of God. What then? Does the resurrection mean
anything for your life *now*? Oh my, yes.

Isaiah, Amos, and many of the prophets wrote about what
God wants to bring about in the future—the kingdom of God,
the new heaven and new earth, a healed material creation: "The
wolf lying down with the lamb; the child playing with the cobra
and adder without fear" (Isaiah 11). Absolute wholeness and
well-being—physically, spiritually, socially, and economically.
When John the Baptist sends a messenger from prison who says
to Jesus in Matthew 11: "Are you really the Messiah? Are you
the one who is bringing the kingdom of God?" Jesus answers:

"The blind receive sight, the lame walk, those who have leprosy are cured, the deaf hear, the dead are raised, and the good news is preached to the poor" (Matthew 11:5). That is the kingdom of God—*shalom*—complete healing of all the relationships in the creation. We will be reconciled to God; to nature; to one another; and to ourselves.

And to the extent that that future is real to you, it will change everything about how you live in the present. For example, why is it so hard to face suffering? Why is it so hard to face disability and disease? Why is it so hard to do the right thing if you know it's going to cost you money, reputation, maybe even your life? Why is it so hard to face your own death or the death of loved ones? It's so hard because we think this broken world is the only world we're ever going to have. It's easy to feel as if this money is the only wealth we'll ever have, as if this body is the only body we'll ever have. But if Jesus is risen, then your future is so much more beautiful, and so much more certain, than that.

Every Easter I think about Joni Eareckson Tada. She was in an accident when she was seventeen, and ever since she has been a quadriplegic, paralyzed from the neck down. While she was still trying to come to terms with this horrible accident, she would go to church in her wheelchair.

The problem with being in a wheelchair, she found, was that at a certain point in her church's liturgy every Sunday, the priest called everyone to kneel—which drove home to her the fact that she was stuck in a wheelchair. Once she was at a convention in which the speaker urged people to get down on their knees and pray. Everyone did except Joni. "With everyone kneeling, I certainly stood out. And I couldn't stop the tears." But it wasn't because of self-pity. She was crying because the sight of hundreds of people on their knees before God was so beautiful—"a picture of heaven." And then she continued weeping at another thought:

> Sitting there, I was reminded that in heaven I will be free to jump up, dance, kick, and do aerobics. And. . . . sometime before the guests are called to the banquet table at the Wedding Feast of the Lamb, the first thing I plan to do on resurrected legs is to drop on grateful, glorified knees. I will quietly kneel at the feet of Jesus.[72]

Then she adds: "I, with shriveled, bent fingers, atrophied muscles, gnarled knees, and no feeling from the shoulders down, will one day have a new body, light, bright, and clothed in righteousness—powerful and dazzling. Can you imagine the hope that the resurrection gives someone who is spinal cord–injured like me?"[73] Only in the gospel of Jesus Christ do people find such enormous hope to live. Only the resurrection promises us not just new minds and hearts, but also new bodies. They are going to be more indissoluble, more perfect, more beautiful. They will be able to be and do and bear the burden of what bodies are supposed to do in a way in which our present bodies cannot.

If you can't dance and you long to dance, in the resurrection you'll dance perfectly. If you're lonely, in the resurrection you will have perfect love. If you're empty, in the resurrection you will be fully satisfied. Ordinary life is what's going to be redeemed. There is nothing better than ordinary life, except that it's always going away and always falling apart. Ordinary life is food and work and chairs by the fire and hugs and dancing and mountains—this world. God loves it so much that he gave his only Son so we—and the rest of this ordinary world—could be redeemed and made perfect. And that's what is in store for us.

And if you know that this is not the only world, the only body, the only life you are ever going to have—that you will someday have a *perfect* life, a real, concrete life—who cares what people do to you? You're free from ultimate anxieties in this life, so you can be brave and take risks. You can face the worst thing, even life in a wheelchair, with joy, with hope. The resurrection means we can look forward with hope to the day our suffering will be gone. But it even means that we can look forward with hope to the day our suffering will be glorious. When Jesus shows the disciples his hands and his feet, he is showing them his scars. The last time the disciples saw Jesus, they thought those scars were ruining their lives. The disciples had thought they were on a presidential campaign. They thought that their candidate was going to win and they were going to be in the cabinet, and when they saw the nails going into the hands and the feet and the spear going into the side, they believed those wounds had destroyed their lives. And now Jesus is showing them that in his resurrected body his scars are still there.

Why is this important? Because now that they understand the scars, the sight and memory of them will increase the glory and joy of the rest of their lives. Seeing Jesus Christ with his scars reminds them of what he did for them—that the scars they thought had ruined their lives actually saved their lives. Remembering those scars will help many of them endure their own crucifixions.

On the Day of the Lord—the day that God makes everything right, the day that everything sad comes untrue—on that day the same thing will happen to your own hurts and sadness. You will find that the worst things that have ever happened to you will in the end only enhance your eternal delight. On that day, all of it will be turned inside out and you will know joy beyond the walls of the world. The joy of your glory will be that much greater for every scar you bear.

So live in the light of the resurrection and renewal of this world, and of yourself, in a glorious, never-ending, joyful dance of grace.

AFTER

As a minister, I've talked over the years to hundreds of people wrestling with issues of faith and doubt. One of the most frequent objections to Christianity that I've heard is that it is "too pat" or "escapist." One man once said to me, "I can understand why people want to come and hear that someday God will make everything better. The stories of the Bible and of Jesus are certainly consoling. But in the end it's all just wishful thinking."

We live in one of the first eras of history in which it is widely believed that a happy ending is the mark of inferior art. Why? Many are certain that, ultimately, life is meaningless and that happy endings are misleading at best. Life therefore would be better represented by paradox, irony, and a sense of frustration. Happy endings are all right for children's stories, perhaps, but not for thinking adults. "Grown-up" art, whether it's *Seinfeld* or *Waiting for Godot,* deliberately lacks narrative coherence and, of course, any happy ending.

Perhaps that is the reason that Steven Spielberg was refused

any Oscars until he stopped making movies with only happy endings, yet his fairy tale-ending movies are his most popular by far.
Critics observe this and scowl that, of course, "escapist" stories
will always be popular.

But no less an authority than Professor J. R. R. Tolkien explains
the abiding popularity of the stories the critics disdain. He insists
that people sense that happy endings are not "escapist" but somehow true to reality. In his famous essay "On Fairy-Stories" Tolkien
expounds his view that the mark of the most satisfying stories is
eucatastrophe. *Katastrophe* is the Greek word for a dramatic, world-
changing turn, but what does Tolkien mean by *eu*-catastrophe?

> [T]he joy of the happy ending . . . is not essentially
> "escapist" nor "fugitive." . . . It does not deny the exis-
> tence of *dyscatastrophe*, of sorrow and failure: the pos-
> sibility of these is necessary to the joy of deliverance
> [*eucatastrophe*]; it denies (in the face of much evidence,
> if you will) universal final defeat, and in so far is *evan-
> gelium*, giving a fleeting glimpse of Joy, Joy beyond
> the walls of the world, poignant as grief. . . . When the
> sudden "turn" comes we get a piercing glimpse of joy,
> and heart's desire, that for a moment passes outside the
> frame, rends indeed the very web of story, and lets a
> gleam come through.[74]

Tolkien goes on to argue that people sense that such stories
point to some underlying Reality. As we read or watch them,
we are being told that the world *is* certainly filled with danger,
sorrow, and tragedy but that nonetheless there *is* a meaning to
things, there *is* a difference between good and evil, and above
all, there *will* be a final defeat of evil and even an "escape from
death"—which Tolkien says is the quintessential happy ending.

In this volume we have traced out the story of Jesus according to Mark, the Gospel-writer. It is a compelling narrative, with vividly drawn characters, surprising and even shocking plot twists, and a cosmic victory miraculously snatched from the jaws of defeat. It's a moving story, but is that all it is? Does the gospel simply give us the temporary emotional lift that all stories with happy endings give us?

No, it gives us much more, and Tolkien himself, in the epilogue to his essay, explains why. In an argument similar to the one that helped persuade his friend C. S. Lewis on Addison's Walk by the River Cherwell in Oxford years before, he argues that the gospel story of Jesus is not simply one more great story, pointing to the underlying Reality.[75] Rather, the gospel story of Jesus *is* the underlying Reality to which all the stories point. It gives us more than a passing inspiration because it is *the* true story; it happened.

> The peculiar quality of the "joy" in a successful Fantasy can be thus explained as a sudden glimpse of the underlying reality or truth. . . . The Gospels contain . . . a story of a larger kind which embraces all the essence of fairy-stories. . . . But this story has entered history and the primary world. . . . The Birth of Christ is the eucatastrophe of Man's history. The Resurrection is the eucatastrophe of the story of the Incarnation. This story begins and ends in joy. . . . There is no tale ever told that men would rather find was true, and none which so many skeptical men have accepted as true on its own merits.

The fact of the resurrection of Jesus is what makes the gospel story not merely a great experience to read, but a life-changing power. Imagine for a moment someone preaching to slaves in the ancient city of Antioch, and imagine him saying, "Ah, the res-urrection is basically just an inspiring story, you know. It means that somehow, good is stronger than evil. So let's be kind to each other." Would it be possible that any of the slaves would say: "Wonderful! This message transforms my life of grinding misery and oppression into one of triumphant hope!" Of course not. But that is not what Paul said when he got to the cities of the Mediterranean. He said, "They *saw* him, and *touched* him. He really rose. That proves that the kingdom of God is real and will triumph. If you believe, you enter his realm and power now."[76] The story of Jesus changes our lives because it is true.

And in no way is the gospel story sentimental or escapist. Indeed, the gospel takes evil and loss with utmost seriousness, because it says that we cannot save ourselves. Nothing short of the death of the very Son of God can save us. But the "happy ending" of the historical resurrection is so enormous that it swal-lows up even the sorrow of the Cross. It is so great that those who believe it can henceforth fully face the depth of the sorrow and brokenness of life. If we disbelieve the gospel, we may weep for joy at the happy ending of some other inspiring story, but the enchantment will quickly fade, because our minds will tell us "life is not really like that." But if we believe the gospel, then our hearts slowly heal even as we face the darkest times because we know that, because of Jesus, life *is* like that. Then even our griefs, even the *dyscatastrophes* we know, will be taken up into the miraculous grace of God's purposes. "Death has been swallowed up in victory. . . . Thanks be to God! He gives us the victory through Jesus Christ" (1 Corinthians 15:54 and 57).

In a famous article, theologian Robert W. Jenson argued that our culture is in a crisis because the modern world "has lost its story."[77] We once thought that life had a purpose, that there was something to live for, and that there was hope for a resolution to the sufferings of the world. Now, many say, none of those things are true.

However, Mark has given us the story of Jesus and declared that this is actually the world's true story as well: Jesus, the King, created all things in love. He has the power and the beauty to see his vision for the world through to its glorious end, to undo everything we have been able to do to harm it. To accomplish that, he had to come and die for it. Three days later, he rose again; and one day will come back again to usher in a renewed creation.

The gospel is the ultimate story that shows victory coming out of defeat, strength coming out of weakness, life coming out of death, rescue from abandonment. And because it is a *true* story, it gives us hope because we know life is really like that.

It can be your story as well. God made you to love him supremely, but he lost you. He returned to get you back, but it took the cross to do it. He absorbed your darkness so that one day you can finally and dazzlingly become your true self and take your seat at his eternal feast.

NOTES

1. Lisa Miller, *Newsweek*, March 25, 2010.
2. Geza Vermes, "Myth or History: The Hard Facts of the Resurrection," *Times of London*, April 6, 2009.
3. Nanci Helmich, *USA Today*, March 23, 2010.
4. Two good surveys of how this skepticism over the Gospels developed are found in Ben Witherington, *The Jesus Quest: The Third Search for the Jew of Nazareth* 2nd ed. (Downers Grove, Illinois: Inter-Varsity Press, 1997) and N. T. Wright, *Who Was Jesus?* (London: SPCK, 1992).
5. For popular level treatments, see C. Blomberg, *The Historical Reliability of the Gospels* (Downers Grove, Illinois: IVP, 1987), Craig A. Evans, *Fabricating Jesus: How Modern Scholars Distort the Gospels* (Downers Grove, Illinois: IVP, 2008) as well as the more popular and older F. F. Bruce, *The New Testament Documents: Are They Reliable?* (Eerdmans, reissued 2003 with a foreword by N. T. Wright). For analysis of these philosophical underpinnings of much skeptical biblical scholarship, see C. Stephen Evans, *The Historical Christ and the Jesus of Faith* (Oxford University Press, 1996), and Alvin Plantinga, "Two (or More) Kinds of Scripture Scholarship" in *Warranted Christian Belief* (Oxford, 2002).

6. A. N. Wilson, "Why I Believe Again," *The New Statesman,* April 2, 2009. Unlike Rice, Wilson's return to faith came not so much from an examination of biblical scholarship as from the weaknesses he saw in the philosophical objections to Christianity. But the *New Statesman* accompanies his article about returning to faith with an ironic picture of Wilson, carrying his skeptical 1992 book about Jesus, yet now looking upward, toward heaven.

7. Anne Rice, *Christ the Lord: Out of Egypt* (New York: Ballantine, 2005), p. 332. While Rice's relationship with the church and institutional Christianity remains complicated, she returned to belief that the Bible gives us a trustworthy portrait of Jesus.

8. See D. A. Carson and Douglas J. Moo, *An Introduction to the New Testament* (Grand Rapids: Zondervan, 2005), p. 173.

9. Emile Cailliet, "The Book That Understands Me," in Frank E. Gaebelein, ed. *A Christianity Today Reader* (Tappan, NJ: Fleming Revell, 1968) p. 22.

10. Ibid., p. 31.

11. C. S. Lewis, *Mere Christianity* (New York: Macmillan, 1977), p. 151.

12. Cornelius Plantinga, *Engaging God's World: A Christian Vision of Faith, Learning, and Living* (Grand Rapids: Eerdmans, 2002), pp. 20–23.

13. Lewis, p. 151.

14. J. R. R. Tolkien, *The Return of the King: Being the Third Part of the Lord of the Rings* (New York: HarperCollins, 2004), p. 1072.

15. C. S. Lewis, *The Last Battle* (1956; repr. New York: HarperCollins, 1994), p. 196.

16. George MacDonald, *The Princess and the Goblin* (London: Blackie and Son, 1888), pp. 155–212.

17. George MacDonald, *Sir Gibbie: A Novel* (Philadelphia: J. B. Lippincott, 1879), p. 149.

18. George MacDonald, *Lilith* (1895; repr. Charleston, SC: BiblioBazaar, 2007), p. 176.

19. Charles Wesley, "And Can It Be That I Should Gain."

20. Reprinted in Cynthia Heimel, *If You Can't Live Without Me, Why Aren't You Dead Yet?* (New York: Grove, 1991), pp. 13–14.

21. C. S. Lewis, *The Voyage of the Dawn Treader* (1952; repr. New York: HarperCollins, 1994), pp. 115–16.

22. N. T. Wright, *For All God's Worth: True Worship and the Calling of the Church* (Grand Rapids: Eerdmans, 1997), p. 1.

23. Richard Bauckham, *Jesus and the Eyewitnesses: The Gospels as Eyewitness Testimony* (Grand Rapids: Eerdmans, 2006), p. 343ff.

24. Quoted in Bauckham, p. 343n.

25. Elisabeth Elliot, *Through Gates of Splendor:* 40th Anniversary Edition (Wheaton, IL: Tyndale, 1981), p. 267.

26. C. S. Lewis, *The Lion, the Witch and the Wardrobe* (New York: Harper-Collins, 1978), p. 81.

27. George MacDonald, *The Princess and the Goblin* (London: Blackie and Son, 1888), p. 223.

28. "How Firm a Foundation," att. John Keith, 1787 (modernized).

29. Jacques Ellul, *The Technological Society,* translated by John Wilkinson (New York: Knopf, 1964).

30. Franz Kafka, *The Basic Kafka* (New York: Pocket, 1984), p. 169. See also Franz Kafka, *The Trial*. Mike Mitchell, translator (New York: Oxford, 2009).

31. Aleksandr Solzhenitsyn, *The Gulag Archipelago* (New York: Harper-Collins, 2002) p. 312.

32. Quoted in Stuart Babbage, *The Mark of Cain: Studies in Literature and Theology* (Grand Rapids: Eerdmans, 1966), p. 17.

33. Quoted in Dorothy Sayers, *Creed or Chaos?* (New York: Harcourt, 1949) p. 39.

34. Ibid., p. 38.

35. Christina Kelly, "Why Do We Need Celebrities?" *Utne Reader* (May/June, 1993), pp. 100–101.

36. The critical study was Anders Nygren, *Commentary on Romans* translated by Carl C. Rasmussen (Philadelphia: Muhlenberg, 1949). See the entry on Romans 1:17. This is also how Martin Luther read this verse, though many modern commentators differ. See the standard *Luthers Werke*, Volume 34, p. 337.

37. Matthew 5:18.

38. James Proctor, "It Is Finished."

39. James R. Edwards, *The Gospel According to Mark* (Grand Rapids: Eerdmans, 2002), p. 221.

40. John Newton, *The Works of the Rev. John Newton,* Volume VI (Edinburgh: Banner of Truth, 1985), p. 185.

41. William Vanstone, *Love's Endeavour, Love's Expense* (London: Darton, Longman and Todd, 1977).

42. Cf. A. M. Stibbs, "Blood is a visible token of life violently ended; it is a sign of life either given or taken in death. Such giving or taking of life is in this world the extreme, both of gift or price and of crime or penalty. Man knows no greater." Quoted in Leon Morris, *The Cross in the New Testament* (Grand Rapids: Eerdmans, 1965), p. 219n21.

43. J. Edwards, *The Gospel According to Mark,* p. 254.

44. See Acts 2:24; 1 Corinthians 15:54–56.

45. C. S. Lewis, *Mere Christianity* (New York: Macmillan, 1958), p. 174.

46. For two commentaries that read this text in this way, see James R. Edwards, *The Gospel According to Mark,* p. 260 (he understands Jesus to be referring to his resurrection), and also D. A. Carson, *Matthew: The Expositors' Bible Commentary* (Grand Rapids: Zondervan, 1995), Volume II, p. 382. Carson reads the Matthean version of this saying as referring to the multiplication of the church.

47. Ibid., p. 175.

48. C. S. Lewis, "The Weight of Glory," in *The Weight of Glory and Other Essays* (New York: Simon and Schuster, 1980), pp. 36–37.

49. Lamin Sanneh, *Whose Religion Is Christianity?* (Grand Rapids: Eerdmans, 2003), p. 15, and Philip Jenkins, *The Next Christendom: The Coming of Global Christianity* (London: Oxford, 2002) p. 56.

50. "The Expansion of Christianity: An Interview with Andrew Walls" was accessed at www.religion-online.org/showarticle.asp?title=2052.

51. J. K. Rowling, *Harry Potter and the Philosopher's Stone* (London: Bloomsbury, 1997), p. 216.

52. C. S. Lewis, *The Lion, the Witch and the Wardrobe* (New York: Collier/Macmillan, 1970), p. 169.

53. Richard Hays, *The Moral Vision of the New Testament: A Contemporary Introduction to New Testament Ethics* (San Francisco: Harper, 1996), p. 90.

54. This image can be viewed online at www.zinzendorf.com/feti.htm.

55. "The Excellency of Jesus Christ" in *The Sermons of Jonathan Edwards: A Reader,* ed. W. H. Kimnach, K. P. Minkema, D. A. Sweeney (New Haven: Yale, 1999), p. 163.

56. The Josephus reference is given in Edwards, *The Gospel According to Mark,* p. 341.

57. Edwards explains that the popular imagination conveniently overlooked the Old Testament references to the temple being a place for the nations to come and worship. See Edwards, *The Gospel According to Mark,* p. 343.

58. The tabernacle was the temple's precursor—a portable sanctuary during Israel's wilderness wanderings.

59. John Owen, *The Death of Death in the Death of Christ.* This seventeenth-century work is available in many printed versions and is also online in its entirety. J. I. Packer's modern "Introduction to the Death of Death in the Death of Christ" is an important short essay in its own right.

60. D. A. Carson, *Love in Hard Places* (Wheaton, IL: Crossway, 2002), p. 61.

61. "The Martyrdom of Polycarp," in Cyril C. Richardson, *Early Christian Fathers* (New York: Macmillan, 1970), p. 153.

62. John Foxe, *Foxe's Book of Martyrs* (New York: Oxford University Press, 2009), p. 154.

63. C. S. Lewis, *Letters to Malcolm: Chiefly on Prayer* (New York: Harcourt, Brace, and World, 1963), pp. 96–97.

64. Jonathan Edwards, "Christ's Agony." This is available in numerous published forms, and is on the Internet at several addresses. It was accessed at www.ccel.org/ccel/edwards/sermons.agony.html.

65. C. John Sommerville, *The Decline of the Secular University* (London: Oxford, 2006), p. 70.

66. Michael Wilcock, *The Message of Luke: The Savior of the World* (Downers Grove, IL: IVP, 1979), p. 86.

67. For example, see Isaiah 13:9,10; Jeremiah 15:6–9.

68. For example, see in Psalm 84:11.

69. Albert Camus' quote is found in Jurgen Moltmann, *The Crucified God* (Minneapolis: Fortress, 1993), p. 226.

70. J. R. R. Tolkien, *The Return of the King* (New York: HarperCollins, 2004), pp. 1148–1149.

71. See chapter *Before* on Bauckham's argument that the Gospels are eye-witness testimony.

72. Joni Earekson Tada, *Heaven: Your Real Home* (Grand Rapids: Zondervan, 1997), p. 51.

73. Ibid., p. 53.

74. J. R. R. Tolkien, *Tree and Leaf* and *The Homecoming of Beorhtnoth* (New York: HarperCollins, 2001), pp. 68–70.

75. See Humphrey Carpenter, *The Inklings: C.S. Lewis, J.R.R. Tolkien, Charles Williams, and their Friends* (Boston: Houghton Mifflin, 1979), pp. 42ff.

76. See 1 Corinthians 15:19–20; Colossians 1:13–14.

77. Robert W. Jenson, "How the World Lost Its Story," *First Things 36* (October 1993), pp. 19–24.

ACKNOWLEDGMENTS

No book arrives in your hands without the efforts of many people besides the author, and this volume more than most.

I want to thank Brian Tart, my editor, for his usual brilliant job of suggesting additions and subtractions. Also, this volume owes an unusual debt to my agent, David McCormick, who in addition to superbly handling his normal agently duties, was also the architect of the agreement creating the Redeemer imprint. This book is the first fruit of that agreement.

Most particularly I want to thank Scott Kauffmann and Sam Shammas, who lead Redeemer's content development efforts. It turns out that transforming material that has been preached as sermons into something meant to be read isn't as easy as you might think—at least, not as easy as I thought.

The book of Mark is perhaps the Gospel I have most studied and preached in the course of my ministry. I have done two sets of small group Bible studies on Mark and preached completely through it at least three times, as well as having drawn on Mark for numbers of stand-alone sermons.

So when the idea of transcribing and publishing the latest of these sermons was suggested, I was confident that the material would merely need some tweaking in order to be ready to print. The more fool I.

Beginning with our old friend Laurie Collins, a court reporter who faithfully transposed the sermons from audio to written form, complete with every um, er, and sentence fragment, and continuing on to our new friend Ruth Goring, the manuscript went through a process intent on combing out all those oral-isms that are barely noticeable when you listen to a sermon but are aggravating to read. However, this left me with a clean yet still somewhat lifeless manuscript that should have been vibrating with the intensity that Mark infused into his Life of Jesus.

It wasn't until the eleventh hour, when Scott and Sam got their hands on the manuscript and worked night and day and night again (under the press of a hard stop deadline) that the written word took on whatever liveliness it presently enjoys. A simple "thank you" isn't enough to cover the sacrifices they made and the help they rendered, so this book is dedicated to them, looking forward to many projects together in the future.

ABOUT THE AUTHOR

TIMOTHY KELLER was born and raised in Pennsylvania, and educated at Bucknell University, Gordon-Conwell Theological Seminary, and Westminster Theological Seminary. He was first a minister in Hopewell, Virginia. In 1989 he started Redeemer Presbyterian Church in Manhattan, with his wife, Kathy, and their three sons. Today, Redeemer has more than five thousand regular Sunday attendees, and has helped to start nearly two hundred new churches around the world. Also the author of *Generous Justice*, *Counterfeit Gods*, *The Prodigal God*, and the *New York Times* bestseller *The Reason for God*, he lives in New York with his family.

REDEEMER

The Redeemer imprint is dedicated to books that address pressing spiritual and social issues of the day in a way that speaks to both the core Christian audience and to seekers and skeptics alike. The mission for the Redeemer imprint is to bring the power of the Christian gospel to every part of life. The name comes from Redeemer Presbyterian Church in New York City, which Tim Keller started in 1989 with his wife, Kathy, and their three sons. Redeemer has begun a movement of contextualized urban ministry, thoughtful preaching, and church planting across America and throughout major world cities.